GHOST SCIENCE

THE ESSENTIAL GUIDE FOR THE SCIENTIFIC STUDY OF GHOSTS & HAUNTINGS

By Vincent Wilson

D1526732

A WHITECHAPEL PRODUCTIONS PRESS PUBLICATION

I would like to thank all the members of MD-PIC, BSPR, Beltsville Ghosts and. Specifically Robbin Van Pelt, Scott Fowler, Mary Duvall, Jaime Lee Henkin, Ryan and Jaime Handley, Mark Nesbitt and Rosemary Ellen Guiley. I would also like to thank Troy Taylor who keeps publishing my books and for being a good friend besides.

I would like to dedicate this book to Renée Colianni for getting me into this and Mary for her support. I would also like to dedicate this book to Kenny, Ciara, Nicky, and Lauren just because they're the best kids in the world and I love them very much. I would also like to mention my brother Francis for no reason at all.

Original Cover Artwork Designed by
Michael Schwab &Troy Taylor
Visit M & S Graphics at www.manyhorses.com

This Book is Published by:
Whitechapel Productions Press
P.O. Box 1190 - Decatur, Illinois - 62525
(217) 422-1002 / 1-888-GHOSTLY
Visit us on the Internet at http://www.prairieghosts.com

First Edition - May 2006
ISBN: 1-892523-45-0

Printed in the United States of America

Haunted Field Guide Series

Welcome to the new book in a continuing series from Whitechapel Productions Press that will be dedicated to providing the readers with "field guides" to not only haunted places, but to ghost research as well. In the books to come, we will continue to take you beyond the edge of the unknown and provide detailed listings, maps and directions to haunted places all over the Midwest and America, plus additional books on ghost research and more!

We hope that you continue to enjoy the series and that you will journey with us in the future as we take you past the limits of hauntings in America and beyond the furthest reaches of your imagination!

Happy Hauntings!

TABLE OF CONTENTS

PREFACE
by Mark Nesbitt

In his first book, *Ghost Tech*, Vince Wilson explained the equipment necessary to detect environmental anomalies that many people believe are the remnants of the dead-in layman's terms, ghosts. Now, in *Ghost Science*, he explores the scientific principles behind why the instruments work to identify the paranormal. By doing so, he presents clues as to why ghosts must exist, why they exist where they do, and how we can find evidence of their spirit essences.

There's a reason why, on a paranormal investigation, Vince Wilson's electromagnetic field (EMF) meters go off, or his digital thermometers register temperatures changes. They react because ghosts obey his maxim, "If you want to exist in the universe, you must obey its rules." For ghosts to exist, they must affect the environment in some way, and when they do, they must be obeying some-albeit obscure, perhaps even as yet unidentified-law of science.

Vince tracks the history of the study of the paranormal and reviews the tangential science that may be the explanation for ghostly encounters. He explains the scientific principles behind energy, and the laws of physics that virtually assure that there is existence of the human spirit after death. His correlation between scientific theory and paranormal experiences provide the information the reader needs to develop his own experiments to potentially prove survival theory-the theory that the soul survives the death of the corporeal body.

--Mark Nesbitt, author,
Ghosts of Gettysburg Series

FOREWORD
by Rosemary Ellen Guiley

I have always believed in ghosts. Not because of any scientific or hard evidence, but because of my own experience of them, from an early age. Now, I didn't experience ghosts all the time or even a lot of time, but I had sufficient events that convinced me of the reality of ghosts. Back then it seemed clear to me that ghosts were the dead making themselves known, and they were as "normal" to me as the living.

Growing up, I was surprised to discover that not all people shared that view. Not everyone experiences a "ghost," and even if they do, they may remain in doubt, turmoil, or even denial as to exactly what it was that they experienced. Ghosts make many people uncomfortable.

As Vince Wilson describes in this book, people have experienced ghosts throughout history. They have always been with us. My own experiences of them have run a gamut of ones commonly had by others. For example, I have had visual sightings, tactile experiences, paranormal smells and sounds, "cold spot" sensations and poltergeist effects. Some of my experiences conform with experiences had by others in the same locations, and some of my experiences are unique to me.

Around the world, we have entertained lots of questions about ghosts, have pondered them, and have formulated definite ideas about what ghosts are and what they are not. But after centuries of experiences and more than a century of scientific investigations, we still do not have definitive answers.

This is not discouraging, however. Far from it. In fact, the elusive nature of ghosts makes them all the more tantalizing. There is much more to a ghost than a sighting or paranormal phenomena.

Ghost investigation has become the most popular field of paranormal inquiry. Armed with increasingly sophisticated technology and enlightened by increasingly sophisticated ideas about the nature of "reality," we keep pushing for that piece of evidence that will prove and explain, once and for all, the realm of ghosts. Are they really the dead? Are they paranormal recordings? Projections of memories of the living? Are they something we can't fathom because we don't yet have the right knowledge? We can experience ghosts, but can science validate them?

For several years, I have had the pleasure of working with Vince in paranormal investigations and research. He is one of the most dedicated researchers in the field, passionate in his pursuit of knowledge and evidence. He is innovative and inventive, always coming up with new ideas and experiments. His first book, *Ghost Tech*, established his leadership in technical expertise.

In *Ghost Science*, Vince explores that tantalizing and elusive territory of "ghost reality," and how science stands to help us understand more about our ghost experiences - as well as other types of paranormal experiences. We need to be flexible in our thinking and very open-minded. Ghost Science opens intriguing avenues that every paranormal researcher should consider.

I mentioned earlier that my first ideas about ghosts were that they are genuinely the dead. Over the course of time, study and experience, I have expanded my own concepts of ghosts, which I briefly explain later in the forum in Ghost Science. I am less certain about definitive explanations, and favor instead probable explanations. Ghosts may not always be the dead, or even recordings related to the dead. Science has already demonstrated that the multiverse - the multidimensional field in which we exist - is dynamic and fluid. A reality is just a thought away. A ghost might be a cocktail of ingredients determined by a host of influences.

Increasingly, I think the living play a co-creative role in all of our experiences, far more so than we might imagine. We are not passive observers of phenomena. How and why we experience ghosts, for example, may have more to do with us than with the "ghosts." We know through our own experiences that intersections between the realms of the living and the dead exist. Exactly what these intersections are, and how and why they function, is still a mystery.

Vince Wilson appreciates all the facets of the ghost puzzle. He knows the need for hard data - the photos, the videos, the tech readings, the stats. He knows the value of personal experience testimony. He also appreciates the mystery, and the open-ended questions that need to be posed. That's why he has written this provocative book.

You'll enjoy *Ghost Science*. It joins *Ghost Tech* as required reading in the paranormal investigator's library.

- Rosemary Ellen Guiley
Author, The Encyclopedia of Ghosts and Spirits

INTRODUCTION

First of all, I want to mention that I will be generalizing the word "ghost" a lot in this book. This is to simplify things. I am going to try to avoid using terms like "phantoms", "shadow people" and the like. Feel free to squiggle out the word ghost and draw a line to a word of your choosing in the margins. Hey, it's your book now... unless you're reading it for free in Barnes & Nobles! Don't write in it unless you plan on buying it!

I did a lot of research for my first book *Ghost Tech*. At one point I had a pile of notes two feet high next to my computer. Even with all that research, *Ghost Tech* wasn't a very large book. I like to think it was still very informative, just not excessively wordy, although, it could have been. I suppose I could have included all of my notes on the science of ghosts and hauntings back then, but the main focus of *Ghost Tech* was the gear used by paranormal investigators. It would not have been fair to the reader if I spent four or five chapters on the what ghosts might be before I even got to the topic of the book. Besides, it was obvious to me later on that the "extra stuff" really did deserve a book of its own.

One of the main purposes of this book is to show that not only do ghosts exist but also that the laws that govern reality allow them. In this book you will see many theories as to what ghosts are and how hauntings are plausible. You will also read about how it might be possible that some people are indeed sensitive to these phenomena.

In Chapter One, we will touch on human bias. That is, how a person's opinion can influence accurate decisions in a ghost investigation or on subjects of the paranormal. Later, I will talk about how human consciences can influence reality itself. Do not get the wrong idea though. These are only theories and conjectures, not solid facts. Just remember for a moment when you were a child and anything was possible. At some point in everyones life, comes a time when you will have to make a choice. Life throws you a curve. This puts beliefs into doubt. Did you continue to believe or did you "grow up"? What did you choose? Well, my friend, I am here to tell you that growing up doesn't mean you have to give up on the interesting stuff.

So, just remember ---- if someone lies to you, don't treat everyone as if they are lying to you too. There are people out there that you can trust and have faith in. Likewise, just because you have never seen a ghost doesn't make everyone out there who has is a kook.

1. DEATH, THE UNIVERSE & EVERYTHING

"I want to know how God created this world. I am not interested in this or that phenomenon, in the spectrum of this or that element. I want to know His thoughts; the rest are details."
-Albert Einstein

Science and ghost hunting do not seem to fit well together, do they? Most skeptics use that against us (we the ghost hunters and specifically those that truly believe in ghosts). Those who study the paranormal and supernatural, (i.e. ghosts & hauntings) are often ridiculed by the scientific community in general and, more specifically, those most influential and infamous skeptics like the flamboy-

The Author is Toast!

ant (and genuinely likeable) James (the Amazing) Randi. Interestingly enough though, and a bit ironic, Randi and those like him seem to believe in nothing at all dealing with the paranormal, supernatural and spiritual to the point it has escalated into a quasi-religion of sorts. They believe in nothing other than what is "scientifically" acceptable to the point it has become a belief system and a paradox in dogma.

Let's turn the tables for a moment shall we? A super-skeptic would argue that a "hard-core" believer in the Catholic religion could believe, or have faith in, in the Virgin Mary to such an extent that they may see Her image in toasted bread (and sell it for a modest sum on eBay!). Ordinary toasted bread with a happenstance likeness to the mother of Christ is a miracle to some.

Likewise, they would argue that an extremely biased believer in the phenomena of ghosts and hauntings would see ghosts in pictures with camera straps and dust particles in front of the lens.

These two examples do indeed happen and they happen quite often. Try as you may to convince the Catholic (we're using an extreme example here! Most Catholics are not that naïve) that it's just toast, they likely won't budge on their opinion; their belief. Likewise, try to convince the would-be ghost hunter that there are just bits of dust in front of his lens and he will shop it around until someone tells him those orbs are indeed ghosts!

Equally dogmatic are the skeptics though. Take a picture of an apparition sitting on a grave in broad daylight with plenty of witnesses around and it's either fraud or a trick of the light *every single time.* No amount of evidence or history will convince them otherwise. Science, they say, is absolute. Well, in their case, this is a very politically correct view of science. Science is absolute, but it is a lot more flexible than Randi and others like him would care to admit.

Ask most skeptics if they are at all interested in seeing evidence that proves the existence of ghosts, hauntings, ESP, etc. and they will probably say "yes". they would love to see proof ---- "As long as it is in a controlled environment." Problem is "bias is as bias does". Go into any experiment believing and expecting a certain result and you will probably get that result. Raise your hand if you think that a truly skeptical person will go into any experiment studying the paranormal not thinking that nothing at all would happen.

As late as the 1960s, scientists were still skeptical that meteorites caused large craters on the moon and on Earth. Many scientists believed the craters were caused by volcanic eruptions here and on the moon. How do we know better now? Someone had a theory, applied the scientific method to that theory, came up with enough proof of that theory that became established as the most likely explanation. In 1963, geologist Eugene Shoemaker wrote a landmark paper on the Barringer Meteorite Crater (or Meteor Crater) in Nevada. Using evidence he collected and then compared with the theories and evidence of other scientists, Eugene was able to convince the scientific community of the validity of meteorite craters. I suppose a meteorite would have to have hit some guy on the head to do the job otherwise.

Suffice it to say, what we need to do is apply science to ghosts and hauntings. This is how scientific advancement is done. So convinced are some that ghosts don't exist they can only use science to try and prove why they can't exist. Why don't they try this, use science to explain how ghosts can exist and then see if you can prove it through experimentation? First, you will need some theories that are scientifically plausible. Ask the question, "If ghosts exist, how?" Then use applied science to test your hypothesis. Nah, that would be too hard and your colleagues might make fun of you, right Professor?

Recently, I tried to do an investigation at a location run by the National Park Service. This particular park will remain nameless except for the blatant clues I am about to leave. They said they weren't interested in ghost research because their only pursuit is that of historic facts. Historic facts? How do we know about history? Yeah, there's evidence like cannon balls and bullets left in the ground. But how do we know someone wasn't trying to plant an iron tree? Well, besides the fact that we hope none of our ancestors could be that dumb and gullible, we learn from eyewitness accounts. We know about the battle at Ft. McHenry during the war of 1812 (the battle happened in 1814) because people like Francis Scott Key were kind enough to tell us about it. The National Park I was trying to investigate was known for eyewitness accounts of ghosts and eerie phenomena. I had to restrain myself from using this example to define the word "hypocrite" in this book's glossary.

Souls: Energy or Figments?

Here's a topic we covered a little in *Ghost Tech*: What are ghosts exactly? Are they:

1. The souls of the deceased trapped on earth?
2. A remnant of deceased persons.
3. A copy of which they were?
4. Psychic projections.
5. So-called "poltergeist agents"?
6. An "astral" projection existing on a higher dimension of reality?
7. A completely magical and ethereal entity outside our ability to comprehend unless you are a shaman of some kind?
8. Demons?
9. Two or more of the above?
10. Other?

An online poll I conducted in June 2005 revealed that, out of over 400 persons (specifically those in the field of ghost hunting) asked, no one believed they were demons, poltergeists, psychic projections or "a completely magical and ethereal entity outside our ability to comprehend unless you are a shaman of some kind." Here are the results:

- The souls of the deceased trapped on earth. 33%
- A remnant of deceased persons. A copy of which they were. 20%
- Psychic projections. 0%
- So-called "poltergeist agents". 0%
- An "astral" projection 13%

- A completely magical and ethereal entity outside our ability to comprehend unless you are a shaman of some kind. 0%
- Demons. 0%
- Two or more of the above. 26%
- Other. 6%

Now, that's not to say that some people who participated in the poll don't believe in a combination of two or more of the above options. However, the poll does suggest that most people in this field believe that ghosts are in fact the souls of the living trapped on earth. That opens a whole new can of worms, huh?

One might argue that options 1 and 7 (and perhaps even option 8) are in fact very related. Aren't souls unexplainable and supernatural? Is the existence of a soul best left to theologians and philosophers? The answer is maybe and maybe not. I am not going to spend any amount of time discussing the existence of God. This book is about ghosts and that's controversial enough. However, I will say this, the laws of the universe that allow us to exist are so perfect that they practically lend themselves to intellectual design. Perhaps you would prefer to believe that we are a big cosmic accident of circumstance.

Most people do believe in ghosts though. A poll conducted in 2003 says that 51% of Americans believe in ghosts. A Gallop poll conducted in June 2005 revealed the following:

June 2005 Poll
Sorted percentage order of "Believe" / "Not Sure About" / "Do Not Believe"

Psychic or spiritual healing or the power of the human mind to heal the body
55 % /17 % /26 %

That people on this earth are sometimes possessed by the devil
42 % / 13 % / 44 %

ESP or Extrasensory Perception
41 % / 25 % / 32 %

That houses can be haunted
37 % / 16 % / 46 %

Ghosts/that spirits of dead people can come back in certain places/situations
32 % / 19 % / 48 %

Telepathy/communication between minds without using traditional senses
31 % / 27 % / 42 %

Clairvoyance/the power of the mind to know the past and predict the future
26 % /24 % / 50 %

Astrology, or that the position of the stars and planets can affect people's lives
25 % / 19 % / 55 %

That extra-terrestrial beings have visited earth at some time in the past
24 % / 24 % / 51%

That people can communicate mentally with someone who has died
21 % / 23 % / 55 %

Witches
21 % / 12 % / 66%

Reincarnation, that is, the rebirth of the soul in a new body after death
20 % / 20 % / 59 %

Channeling/allowing a 'spirit-being' to temporarily assume control of body
9 % / 20 % / 70%

A special analysis of the data shows that 73% of Americans believe in at least one of the 10 items listed above, while 27% believe in none of them. A Gallup survey in 2001 provided similar results -- 76% professed belief in at least one of the 10 items. The poll shows no statistically significant differences among people by age, gender, education, race, and region of the country. Christians are a little more likely to hold some paranormal beliefs than non-Christians (75% vs. 66%, respectively), but both groups show a sizeable majority with such beliefs. Results in the survey are based on telephone interviews with 1,002 national adults, aged 18 and older. For results based on the total sample of national adults, one can say with 95% confidence that the maximum margin of sampling error is +/- 3 percentage points.

When looked a little closer, the Gallop poll contradicts my amateur online poll a bit. While 32% of Americans believed the spirits of the dead (i.e. souls) could come back under certain circumstances, 37% believed a house could be haunted. That suggests that between 2 and 8 percent of those who believe in haunted houses do not believe in the ability of the soul to return to the world of the living. What's even more interesting that is that in a recent survey (2003) of cell phone users taken via text messaging 43.1% of 38,906 participants claim that they have experienced a ghostly or unexplained paranormal experience.

So, what's the point? The point is, that after thousands of years of "development", people still believe in ghosts!

A History of Proof

Opinions have changed on many things over the centuries.

-   The shape of the Earth: Not flat
-   The Earth's composition: Not hollow.
-   The orbits of the planets: We're not the center after all.

In the past, humans used beliefs in spirits and deities to explain things like storms and demons to explain illness and disasters. When lightning and thunder filled the air it was Thor with his mighty hammer for the Norse and Zeus with his, well, thunder bolts for the Greeks. If you were sick for no obvious reason, you may be possessed by demons. If weather and illness had natural explanations, then what about ghosts? When a deceased loved one visits a person in the night and tells him goodbye was as common in the past as it is today. What explanation is there for that? Methinks it cannot be blamed on the weather.

Every culture that has existed in recorded history has some belief in an afterlife. Complex burial techniques and symbolic gestures hint that even prehistoric man believed in life after death. The majority of these cultures also allotted for the existence of a way for the dead to return to the world of the living. You know, those things called ghosts! Egyptian mothers even had cute little nursery songs to sing their children to sleep.

Oh, a vaunt! Ye ghosts of night,
nor do my baby harm;
ye may come with steps so light,

But I'll thwart you with my charm.
For my babe you must not kiss,
nor rock if she should cry--
Oh! If you did aught amiss,

My own, my dear, would die.
O ye dead men, come not near--
Now I have made the charm--
There's lettuce to prick you here,
Garlic with smell to harm;

There 's tow to bind like a spell,
the magic bones are spread;
There's honey the living love well--
'Tis poison to the dead.

How sweet!

Belief in ghosts goes back even further still! In the Epic of Gilgamesh, a story from ancient Babylonia around 2500 B.C. (over 4,000 years ago!!), there is a bit on ghosts mentioned.

The desert oasis even when no rain falls. "My god," he cried, "when death called for me, my best friend went in my place and he is now no longer living." And Ea, whose waters keep us alive as we journey over desert sands, said this to Nergal, great soldier in arms. "Go now, mighty follower; free Enkidu to speak once to kin and show this Gilgamesh how to descend halfway to Hell through the bowels of earth."

And Nergal, accustomed to absurd orders, obeyed as soldiers do and he freed Enkidu to speak once to kin and showed Gilgamesh how to descend halfway to Hell through the bowels of earth. Enkidu's shadow rose slowly toward the living and the brothers, tearful and weak, tried to hug, tried to speak, tried and failed to do anything but sob. "Speak to me please, dear brother," whispered Gilgamesh.

"Tell me of death and where you are." "Not willingly do I speak of death," said Enkidu in slow reply. "But if you wish to sit for a brief time, I will describe where I do stay." "Yes," his brother said in early grief. "All my skin and all my bones are dead now. All my skin and all my bones are now dead. "Oh no," cried Gilgamesh without relief. "Oh no," sobbed one enclosed by grief.

Even ancient Mesopotamia (can you say, "5000 B.C!") had some ghost stories that have survived the passage of time. Advancement after advancement in human history has not stayed the belief in life after death and the existence of ghosts. Opinions have changed, empires have arisen and fallen, technologies have advanced and even in the age of the Forever Flashlight (The Forever Flashlight uses no batteries or bulbs. Instead it uses Faraday's Principle of Induction and a bright LED to produce light without batteries. The light is shaken for about 30 seconds to recharge a capacitor and it will then provide about 5 minutes of light. As the light is shaken, a magnet passes through a metal coil generating electricity. During prolonged use it can be shaken for 10-15 seconds every 2 or 3 minutes. Act now and get a second pocket light for FREE!!) PEOPLE STILL BELIEVE IN G-H-O-S-T-S! Nay, people still SEE ghosts!

A Roman Letter-writer named Pliny the Younger (pictured) who lived from A.D. 61-115 tells of an eyewitness account of an ancient ghost with a message, one not uncommon even today. William Melmoth translated this version

in 1746. I love this story because it may the first to use "rattling chains" and yet it is told as non-fiction.

There was in Athens a house, spacious and open, but with an infamous reputation, as if filled with pestilence. For in the dead of night, a noise like the clashing of iron could be heard. And if one listened carefully, it sounded like the rattling of chains. At first the noise seemed to be at a distance, but then it would approach, nearer, nearer, nearer. Suddenly a phantom would appear, an old man, pale and emaciated, with a long beard, and hair that appeared driven by the wind. The fetters on his feet and hands rattled as he moved them.

Any dwellers in the house passed sleepless nights under the most dismal terrors imaginable. The nights without rest led them to a kind of madness, and as the horrors in their minds increased, onto a path toward death. Even in the daytime--when the phantom did not appear--the memory of the nightmare was so strong that it still passed before their eyes. The terror remained when the cause of it was gone.

Damned as uninhabitable, the house was at last deserted, left to the spectral monster. But in hope that some tenant might be found who was unaware of the malevolence within it, the house was posted for rent or sale.

It happened that a philosopher named Athenodorus came to Athens at that time. Reading the posted bill, he discovered the dwelling's price. The extraordinary cheapness raised his suspicion, yet when he heard the whole story, he was not in the least put off. Indeed, he was eager to take the place. And did so immediately.

As evening drew near, Athenodorus had a couch prepared for him in the front section of the house. He asked for a light and his writing materials, and then dismissed his retainers. To keep his mind from being distracted by vain terrors of imaginary noises and apparitions, he directed all his energy toward his writing.

For a time the night was silent. Then came the rattling of fetters. Athenodorus neither lifted up his eyes, nor laid down his pen. Instead he closed his ears by concentrating on his work. But the noise increased and advanced closer till it seemed to be at the door, and at last in the very chamber. Athenodorus looked round and saw the apparition exactly as it had been described to him. It stood before him, beckoning with one finger.

Athenodorus made a sign with his hand that the visitor should wait a little, and bent over his work. The ghost, however, shook the chains over the philosopher's head, beckoning as before. Athenodorus now took up his lamp and followed. The ghost moved slowly, as if held back by his chains. Once it reached the courtyard, it suddenly vanished.

Athenodorus, now deserted, carefully marked the spot with a handful of grass and leaves. The next day he asked the magistrate to have the spot dug up. There they found--intertwined with chains--the bones that were all that remained of a body that had long lain in the ground. Carefully, the skeletal relics were collected and given proper burial, at public expense. The tortured ancient was at rest. And the house in Athens was haunted no more.

I am often asked by Christians (I am Christian myself) if ghosts have any place in Christian theology. Some Christians claim that ghosts have no place in their belief system. They must not read the Bible very often!

Never mind the Father, Son and Holy Ghost, what about Saul and the witch of Endor?

According to the Old Testament in Samuel: 28:7-16 when David, the slayer of Goliath, took an army up against Saul, king of the Israelites, Saul decided he needed some advice from his predecessor. To bad Samuel was already dead! So, going against the Law of Moses (which forbid necromancy and sorcery) Saul contacted a "medium". King Saul's ser-

vants told the king of a soothsayer or witch in the area known as Endor. In disguise, so as not to alarm the witch, Saul sought her out and asked to speak to Samuel. The witch brought forth "from below" the spirit of Samuel. Boy, was Samuel peeved! He refused to help Saul since Saul had lost faith in God and never listened to Samuel when he was alive in the first place! The next day, David kicked Saul's butt in a very fatal way.

Ghosts have appeared in many cultures and regions around the world. In fact you would be hard pressed to not find stories on ghosts from any culture.

In Islam they believe in the *ifrit* or ghost. Ghosts can also be found in all Asian cultures. For whatever reason many Japanese ghosts have no legs. Instead their lower parts are engulfed in flame. India has many stories of the goings on of ghosts as do African and South American cultures.

A more modern affair in the United States takes place a scant 189 years ago, as of this writing. The famous (or infamous) Bell Witch of Adams, Tennessee has captivated the imaginations of historians and ghost enthusiasts alike. Events occured at the home of John and Lucy Bell that make the Amityville Horror (a probable hoax) look like a story by Dr. Seuss. As a matter of fact, at least three movies have been made on this case in the last two years as of the writing of this book! Opinions vary on what exactly happened at the Bell House but one thing's for sure Scooby; something freaky was going on. ZOINKS!

An angry ghost that came to be known as "Kate" or, more commonly, "the Bell Witch", tormented the Bells and their children. There were noises like scratching, gnawing and banging coming from the walls. Later, covers were pulled from the beds of family members. Hands were slapped and hair pulled. In some story, the Bells' 12 year-old daughter, Betsy was even bruised and bled as if stuck with pins. The problems escalated further still when the ghost began to whistle and even talk! When the townspeople got wind of all this craziness they knew it could only be a witch.

Eventually, even Andrew Jackson became involved. Jackson, a family friend of the Bells, showed up with an "exorcist" and his carriage became stuck in the mud. In one version of the tale Jackson was struck to the floor when he said he didn't believe in "ha'nts" (what we call ghosts).

For more information on this incredible true haunting, read Troy Taylor's *Season of the Witch, History & Hauntings of the Bell Witch of Tennessee*, also from Whitechapel Press.

Even in these modern 21st century times, people still say they see ghosts and experience hauntings. As a ghost investigator (or phasmatologist --- I like that word, it sounds so scientific) I have been privy to dozens of people who have witnessed paranormal phenomena. Many of these people have careers and family and no history whatsoever of mental illness. Most have everything to lose by fabricating a "ghost story". What if their neighbors or co-workers found out? What if (gasp!) property values went down? Why would perfectly normal, everyday people make up such things? Often there are other witnesses like friends and relatives who experience these strange occurrences. There are centuries of evidence and yet some people refuse to acknowledge the existence, or even the possibility of the existence, of ghosts. Why? Eh, who cares why they refute it? I could list a dozen or more explanations why the scientific community in general take the extreme skeptical approach, but I'm not going to. This book is about the theories regarding how ghosts could exist. As stated before, evidence suggests that ghosts exist and too much focus has been made on why they can't be.

Memory Possession

Have you ever heard a ghost story where a guy walks down a flight of stairs and suddenly feels an icy hand give him a shove? How about the sensation someone feels of a cold breath down the back of his or her neck? Did you ever walk into a room and have a feeling of dread, sadness and/or some other emotional response? Many haunted locations have areas in them that have brought about human experiences like these. Are these ghosts or the effects of ghosts? Is that a specter touching your arm? Is that the ghost of the living past giving you a shove or breathing on your neck? On the other hand, maybe you're being possessed!

Now, I am not saying a "Linda Blair thing" is going on here. There are no demons in this theory or even ghosts necessarily. What I am proposing is something I like to call memory possession. Is a ghost pushing you down the stairs or are you reliving the sensation of someone else being pushed down the stairs? Ah! Now that's an interesting spin isn't it?

Many experienced ghost investigators agree that there exists a phenomenon called a *residual haunting*. As defined in the *Ghost Tech Glossary*:

Residual Haunting: probably the most common type of haunting; this is best described as an imprint on the environment; a moment in time, burnt onto the surroundings of a specific location; playing out roles and situations over and over again for centuries at a time; most researchers compare this to a looped video that repeats itself forever; in these cases you might hear footsteps and other strange noises; however, if you see the event being played out, you will not be able to interfere; the "ghosts" here are not conscience of their surroundings; they may not be sentient.

In a residual haunting, the ghosts are not necessarily conscience beings, merely an imprint that has somehow managed to make an impression on the environment so that events of the past repeat themselves over and over again. What if those imprints were so strong that, not only could you see these events and actions played out, but also you could experience the events as a participant? You are literally possessed by the events of the past. Most of the time this is manifested as a sensation like that of an icy hand on the arm or powerful emotions. Some who have experienced the strong emotions of a haunting will weep uncontrollably or become angry and confrontational. In extreme circumstances they will even, over time, change in character. Others have claimed they were a person in the past for a few moments and could even see a battle take place as a soldier on the field. That's silly though. Memory possession? Nothing like that exists in the scientific or medical fields after all. Bah! ...Oh, wait a minute!

It is a fact in the field of medicine that some recipients of organ or limb transplants have acquired the memories of the previous owner without knowing any data on the previous organ/limb owner! Evidence exists of there being atomic systemic memory, molecular systemic memory and cellular systemic memory. In these cases, donor recipients will acquire new tastes and personality traits as well as unfamiliar memories and/or nightmares. The 1997 book titled *A Change of Heart: A memoir of Claire Sylvia* by Claire Sylvia and William Novak documents such a case. The true-life story tells the tale of a woman who's appetites and fashions changed after receiving a new heart and lung. A health nut, Sylvia suddenly found herself craving KFC. The donor was found with the Colonel's special recipe nuggets in his pockets. In another incident, a young black violinist dies in a drive-by shooting. His heart goes to a 47 year-old white construction worker who suddenly finds he loves listening to classical music. Some people who receive transplants from those of the opposite sex will actually change sexual preferences!

One of the most famous instances of this phenomenon is that of a young boy who kept experiencing nightmares involving a man who would chase him and then try to kill him. It turns out that the previous owner of his "new" heart was murdered by the man in his dreams. Later, a description given by the boy helped find the murderer!

Some medical researchers believe that information can be sent electro-magnetically between the brain and the heart. Through electromagnetic resonance information from the donor is sent to the recipient's brain. Could this explain what happens in residual hauntings? Could an electromagnetic signature be imprinted on the environment? In some cases, maybe, the room is the tape and we are the tape players.

Systems Theory is a field of study that covers several scientific fields on the abstract organization of phenomena, regardless of their substance, type, or when or where they exist. It investigates both the principles common to all complex entities, and the models that can be used to describe them. Researchers in the 1940s were the first to seriously suggest that all systems based in reality are open, and interact with, their environments causing changes in both. Dynamical energy systems theory suggests that all dynamical systems store information and energy to various degrees. All I can think of is a bunch of nerds in tie-dyed lab coats sitting around existentially describing Karma. "Dude! Dr. McKenzie looks like Buddha!"

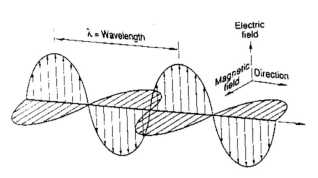

Anyway, an area (any area, albeit a room, house, battlefield, etc.) can acquire an electromagnetic resonance (EMR). If this EMR is on the same, or close to the same, wavelength and frequency as that of the human brain, then perhaps they can influence the electrically stimulated proteins of the human brain that store memory. (Okay, now read that over three more times so you got it, all right?) Under the right circumstances the EMR of an area can overlap memories stored in the brain's synapses. If this were true than that would certainly explain my memory possession theory. I wonder though, could it explain other haunting phenomena as well?

2. MORE ON MAGNETIC ATTRACTIONS

"Magnetism is one of the Six Fundamental Forces of the Universe, with the other five being Gravity, Duct Tape, Whining, Remote Control, and The Force That Pulls Dogs Toward The Groins Of Strangers."
- Dave Barry (American writer and humorist)

EMF Fields and the Dead

From *Ghost Tech*:

Gravity. Most people think it's pretty strong. "Do you understand the gravity of the situation?" That is supposed to imply the seriousness of a given situation as if what could be more serious. Gravity can kill after all. Fall out of an airplane and you are in big trouble without a parachute buddy. How strong is it really though? What would you say if I told you that it's the weakest of the four forces? Think about it. The Earth weighs about 5.972 sextillion (5,972,000,000,000,000,000,000) metric tons. All that mass and all you have to do is put a refrigerator magnet over a paper clip and ta-da: gravity is defied.

Now electromagnetism, there's a powerful force. It's everywhere. It's around you and inside of you. You even emit it. Your cell phone, your car, your TV and your CD player all put out electromagnetic waves. The computer I am typing this on and the coffee maker keeping me awake both put out electromagnetic waves. They are even coming from outer space! It's everywhere! Don't worry though, you're use to it. The earth puts off more electromagnetism than those power lines over your house. You're not going to get a tumor from your cell phone either. Oh, and those bracelets that claim to heal you because they use electromagnetism? Uh-uh, isn't going to happen. Electromagnetism is the bond that keeps your soda carbonated and your molecules together. Appreciate it for what it is.

So, do ghosts give off electromagnetic fields (EMF)? Maybe.

I am still not sure if ghosts actually emit electromagnetic waves. However, the theory I am working on is that they may be electromagnetic waves. Actually, I am suggesting that they are some sort of electromagnetic resonance or EMR. Now, this theory may possibly explain memory possession and residual hauntings to some degree, but what about classic hauntings?

From the *Ghost Tech* Glossary:

Classic Haunting: also called an "Intelligent Haunting" or "Traditional Haunting"; rare, a sentient spirit that can manifest itself into an apparition and communicate with the living; the ghost responds to outside stimuli like questions and statements; it can be friendly or hostile and will let you know the difference; they are sometimes capable of opening and closing doors and windows and moving objects like furniture around.

Here is where the theory gets really complicated! Wait! Don't close the book yet! You're smart --- you can keep up.

Perhaps in the right environment, when someone passes on (you know, drops dead), they can leave an imprint on the area in question in the form of an EMR. Our brains mostly pick up this imprint as a repeating pattern. We may feel strong emotions, experience flashbacks, and feel the memory of someone being pushed or shoved. We may even see events from the past being played out in front of us. If the sensation is strong enough, we can actually experience the events of the past as if we were eyewitnesses. Smells, sites and sounds are all clear to us as if it were happening now. However, like Turner Classic Movies, it's the same thing over and over. In the case of an intelligent haunting, perhaps more than an imprint is left behind. How about an entire copy?

Inside of a tape recorder are two electromagnets that receive a signal from a microphone and translate the signal into a magnetic flux (a measure of the strength of a magnetic field over a given area) that is "remembered" on one half of the tape as a stereo audio signal when it spools by at 4.76 cm per second. When you make a copy of a tape for a friend (You pirate! I'm calling the FCC!), you are repeating the magnetic flux from one tape onto another. Maybe when the conditions are right not only can the events of the past be saved into an area via EMR, but a copy of a person's mind! Like copying a computer hard-drive, the memories that make up the human consciousness can survive after death! However, this would be very rare indeed. Also, the ability to gain additional memories for an EMR ghost would be impaired. They may be capable enough to answer questions in an EVP experiment, but unable to remember it later. Once dead, your ghost would be a copy of you as you were at the moment of death, never changing or evolving or learning. As a ghost you can interact with your environment but never remember any new experiences. You would be PLAY ONLY, never RECORD. This would explain why a civil war era ghost never asks what rap music is. I guess it's not so bad after all.

But what about cases in which objects are physically moved? Now, I imagine that in most cases when someone says that the ghost keeps hiding their keys, the resident homeowner is actually losing the keys and blaming it on the poor ghost in the house. However, reports of floating objects and the like are too numerous to dismiss. An electromagnetic field is the field of force associated with electric charge in motion. It has both electric and magnetic components and contains a definite amount of electromagnetic energy. If acted upon by a, currently unknown, form of EMR reactions, perhaps some of the energy can be converted into kinetic energy (energy possessed by a body in motion) and be released in the form of an object being tossed or moved about.

Since we are only speculating here, perhaps the ghost can "manifest" a reproduction of the electromagnetic field that all solid matter uses to be, well... solid. This could be how some ghosts are capable of being photographed and seem to lift objects on their own. Possessing only a "shell" that looks like the ghost as it did in life, but containing no organs or muscles. This would explain why some ghosts appear transparent or "mist-like". A "residual self image" of the ghost in question that may or may not be self (i.e. the ghost) generated. Now, imagine yourself for a moment. Picture yourself as someone else might see you. Are you picturing your whole self? If you didn't, maybe some ghosts can't or won't either. Hence, the ghosts who appear to have no legs!

Why Ghost Hunters Use EMF Meters

How many times have you seen ghost hunters on television use EMF meters like they were Egon's PKE meter from *Ghostbusters*? I'm sure it's way too many times to count on one hand. They wave the meter around like a once cocaine-addled Robbin Williams (remember when he was funny?) and claim every beep or click is a spirit. Devices like the Trifield Meter and Gaussmaster do not detect ghosts. They detect variations in electromagnetic fields. The Trifield meter is so sensitive (particularly the Natural Trifield Meter) that it can detect the geomagnetic field of the Earth! That means every time someone waves one of these things around like they're swatting flies with it, they're actually detecting the variance between east and west. But they'll say it's a ghost for the listening audience. Actually, it's more because they didn't read the instructions or maybe didn't understand them.

As I stated in my previous book, if you exist in the universe you must obey its rules! No matter what ghosts are or what laws there are which allow them to exist, they must obey the same laws that govern reality in our part of the universe. If they didn't obey those laws then they would be a monkey wrench in the gears that are the principles that govern time and space and reality itself.

When a ghost enters a room or any area, it has to influence that area in some way. In this chapter, we are speculating that they influence electromagnetic fields. When we, as ghost hunters, enter a room with any type of EMF meter we are seeing if any naturally occurring electromagnetic (EM) fields are being disturbed by the presence of ghosts. For information on the proper use of EMF meters and what different types there are, please my first book - *Ghost Tech*! If you were lucky you purchased this book bundled with the other.

EVP: Voices Without Vocal Cords

I was in a haunted mansion in a remote part of Maryland with Mark Nesbitt (author of The *Ghosts of Gettysburg* Series and *The Ghost Hunter's Field Guide: Gettysburg and Beyond*) and Patrick Burke (president of The American Battlefield Ghost Hunter's Society <ABGHS>) and a team of investigators (including Scott Fowler president of Beltsville Ghosts and Daryl "Smitty" Smith of ABGHS) when I experienced some of the most amazing EVP (Electronic Voice Phenomena) yet.

Mark was using a digital recorder on the uppermost floor of the mansion. He was conducting the third part in the ASQ technique for conducting EVP experiments. In part three of ASQ, you ask questions of the ghosts who may be present.

ASQ (pronounced "ask"): the three phases of an EVP investigation. **Alone. Supervise. Ask.**

1.   Leave the recorder **alone** until the tape runs out.
2.   **Supervise** the recording area while it records.
3.   **Ask** questions to check for an intelligent haunting.

Mark started by asking a few questions in regards to the family that once lived there years ago. In this instance, the recorder was in his hand. He would ask if a certain family member was there and then wait three of his breaths for an answer, or about 15 seconds. If the ghost was answering, you were able to see the red indicator LED on the recorder blink. It blinked often that evening.

We asked Mark if he wouldn't mind placing the recorder on a tabletop so to prove for the records, that his hand was not interfering with the recorder. It was not. The light blinked and responses were recorded. But how is this possible? How can a ghost, that is usually assumed to be somewhat intangible, create sounds that can be interpreted as EVP? Let's hypothesis some more, shall we? But first, we will need to know how the human voice works. Hey, I'm not big fan biology either, but bear with me.

Creating the sounds that we call our voice is very complicated. It is one of the miracles of human biology, or in the case of Gilbert Godfrey, a curse. The most important parts of our vocal anatomy are the larynx and the vocal cords. The process of voicing your opinion (or reading this out loud) requires you to move air up from your lungs and past the edges of your vocal cords. This vibrates the loosely touching folds of the vocal cords. The regular air movement causes the fold to open and then snap back. This excites the larynx creating a tonal sound.

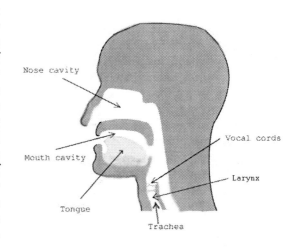

The series of events will repeat itself 110 times a second for the average male and 200 times a second for the average female (there are several very sexist jokes in there that I refuse to touch). The tones created by your larynx and vocal cords are formed into words by your lips in conjunction with your tongue controlling the passage of air. Of course, none of these would be any use without any air. Not only would you be dead from asphyxiation but your last words would go unheard without the medium to carry them: air.

Sound is a sequence of waves of pressure. In order for sound to be heard, it must be transmitted through a medium that will carry it to our eardrums. Sound speed in air is normally 1,130 feet per second at 68° F. Imagine a rock dropped from an outstretched arm into a sandbox. When the rock reaches the sand, it will create a series of ripples from the shockwave emitted from the impact. Likewise, if we drop the rock into a pool of water the water will ripple out from the spot where the rock impacted and broke the water's surface. Without a medium to transmit the vibrations of a sound wave, sound cannot reach our ears or even be recorded via normal means to a recorder, albeit tape or digital medium.

Most every microphone that is readily available to the general public is a *dynamic microphone*. A dynamic microphone uses a thin plastic diaphragm that when introduced to sound vibrations vibrate a magnetic element and coil that, by changes in the positions of the coil and magnetic mass, sends an electric signal to the tape recorder. The microphone that is built into most tape recorders is usually a dynamic microphone. The best dynamic microphones are Neodymium dynamic microphones. They are more sensitive, smaller and more powerful.

Whether or not ghosts can generate the needed sound vibrations to vibrate the diaphragm in a microphone is unknown. It is possible they can directly influence the magnet and coil through electromagnetic energy. Perhaps the same electromagnetic energy that sets off EMF meters.

So, how can a ghost, that has no tangible vocal system, create the necessary sound vibrations to be recorded on an electronic device? Most times, the investigators present during an EVP experiment cannot hear anything but their own breathing. Taking it for granted that the before mentioned theory that ghosts can manifest a shell of electromagnetic energy is true, perhaps they can also manipulate enough of this force field to vibrate the elements of the microphone. The ghost would do all this without thought of course. I'm sure everyone doesn't become an electronics engineer when they die. There is another possibility though.

Perhaps the ghost uses electromagnetic resonance to manipulate the magnetic coils of the microphone. Possibly what happens is a ghost sends out a magnetic pulse that effects the coils much like sound vibrations do. This is an interesting concept, but how can it be tested?

In a *vacuum*!

If a ghost uses EMFs (Electromagnetic Fields) to manipulate the magnetic elements inside a microphone as apposed to vibrating a diaphragm (which is how sound is carried normally) then air would not be necessary to record EVP.

So, here is how the experiment will work.

Using a basic bell jar (the kind you would get from a scientific parts distributor) placed on top of a vacuum pad and hooked to a vacuum pump, we run a microphone into the jar through a rubber stopper placed through the plughole on the top of the bell jar. You can use grease or petroleum jelly to make sure you have a tight fit, but a properly measured stopper should do just fine. Then all you have to do is pump out the air and leave the setup in a location (preferably a known haunted one) to see if you record EVP. Easy and makes a great science project for the kids!

If you record any voices during the experiment you know it must be a ghost since no sound vibration could possibly be reaching the microphone.

Photos and a more detailed how-to for this experiment can be found at the official Ghost Tech website at **www.ghosttech.net**. Also, see the diagram on the next page.

NOTE: After the initial writing of the experiment for the book, extensive experimenting has been done with this setup. I recommend purchasing a metal vacuum pump or brake-bleeding pump (same thing) instead of the plastic ones that are available on some websites. Also, use an empty pickle jar instead of a bell jar to put a small micro-cassette recorder in or digital recorder. You would think an external microphone is not needed for this experiment since vibrations from winding gears cannot be heard anyway, however I have detected an electric hum from an Olympus digital recorder and the same hum from a Panasonic. So, I recently purchased a small external microphone that fits perfectly in the pickle jar I have been using. The microphone is normally used for lecturing and fits on your shirt or lapel.

Why use a pickle jar? The top of the jar is shaved off to be level for a more secure seal. I did manage to find a decorative bowl used to put over dried flower displays. It was cool because it made the experiment look like a crystal ball! However, my cat Teddy knocked that over and broke it. He's fine though and I have no idea why I even bothered to mention that.

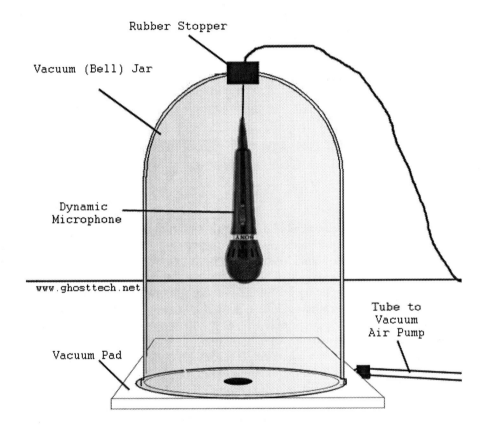

3. COLD RECEPTIONS

1. You cannot win (that is, you cannot get something for nothing, because matter and energy are conserved).

2. You cannot break even (you cannot return to the same energy state, because there is always an increase in disorder; entropy always increases).

3. You cannot get out of the game (because absolute zero is unattainable).

- British scientist and author C.P. Snow in regards to the Laws of Thermodynamics.

The Maryland Paranormal Investigators Coalition believes they have created the most comprehensive set of forms yet for investigating ghosts and hauntings. If you go to **www.ghosttech.net** you can download these forms for free. On the main cover form, you will see spots reserved for Temperature, Barometer Readings, Relative Humidity, Wind Speed (if an outdoor haunting or haunted wind tunnel), Lunar Cycle, Solar Radiation, Geomagnetic Fields and a spot for any other weather or environment notes. Room Data and Information Form #1 has spots for Electromagnetic Fields, Electric Fields and RF (Radio Frequency) Readings. Room Data and Information Form #2 has fields to fill out for Cold Spots, Strange "Feelings" and a spot for "Other".

We also have forms for Video Data Logging and a photo log sheet, along with Room and outdoor Area Grid forms to draw details of the surrounding area in relation to north and south. We print these forms out using a dot matrix (otherwise known as an "impact printer) on non-carbon two-ply paper so we will have two copies for our records. All collected data is filed according to location. Reference tabs for residential owners are created as well. Yeah, that's pretty comprehensive all right.

So what's with all the data collecting?

Nobody knows the how or why of ghosts. We can speculate with theories like the ones in this book, but we're not sure yet. Although I have said it before, I will say it again, when we use our equipment (EMF meters, thermal scanners, etc.) we are not using these devices to detect ghosts! We are looking for the presence of ghosts from how they affect the environment around them. I repeat, "If you want to exist in the universe, you have to obey its rules." All the forces and elements in the universe work as they do because of a specific set of laws. It is a near perfect setup that keeps the sun hot, the water wet and our molecules together. Add in too many ingredients to the cosmological recipe and you get a universe full of really hot soup. And not the good old fashioned chicken noodle soup like mom used to make, no, a primordial soup of subatomic particles just not being able to form into complex matter.

Suffice to say, if we take it for granted that ghosts do exist, we must also take it for granted that they affect the environment in which they haunt. These effects are therefore measurable. Some of the measurable effects that ghosts create include one that doesn't even require fancy equipment: the cold spot!

Thermodynamics Simplified

There are three laws in thermodynamics (the study of energy):

1. Energy cannot be created or destroyed; it can only be converted from one form to another.

2. All systems tend toward disorder. This is one of the principles of Chaos Theory as well (Read *Jurassic Park* for more on this. The book, not the movie!)

3. All molecular movement stops at absolute zero, but absolute zero is unattainable because of the second law.

Early believers in "life after death" used the first law as proof of the existence of life after death: energy cannot be destroyed. Energy can be dissipated however. Skeptics argued that you are still nonexistent after death since your sense of self has dissipated into the atmosphere in a hopelessly scrambled collection of particles. Since we still do not know what happens to your sense of self after death, this is a hopelessly arrogant argument. I like to think that ghost hunters and paranormal investigators deal with possibilities. Skeptics deal in absolutes. Okay, enough skeptics bashing! I try to be "optimistically" skeptic after all. It's just the absolute skepticism that I do not like.

Kinetic energy is the energy of a moving object. This is usually expressed as thermal energy. When the molecules of a given object become excited they will become warmer the more the molecules are excited until the object becomes hot. Energy that is stored is called *Potential energy*. An aerosol can is full of potential energy. When you press the release button on the can you release the stored energy into the environment. The stored energy leaves the can and the can feels cold. Cold air occurs because when the contents of the can are released the inside of the can becomes less excited from the lack of its chemical contents.

Many ghost hunters today believe that ghosts that are manifesting themselves cause cold spots. Energy drawn from the air in one spot is transferred into kinetic energy. This leaves the spot in question with a lower temperature than the surrounding area. Hence cold spots are locations that may signify the presence of a ghost.

Since we do not know how much energy is required to manifest activity for a ghost it is hard to speculate how much colder a cold spot is.

When I look at the directions for my Natural EMF Trifield Meter it tells me this device is so sensitive it can measure an electric field as low as 3 V/m (volts per meter). It says, "A 3V/m field is so feeble that if a 10'x10'x10' room were filled with a field of this strength, it would contain the total amount of energy equivalent to that required to lift a single grain of table salt 1/50th of an inch." Suffice to say it would take thousands of V/m to lift a 3"x5" picture from a dresser and drop it on the floor. This might explain why in some cases of hauntings lights and other electronics will flicker. The ghost in question may be drawing power from the home power as well.

In order to detect cold spots I recommend using two thermometers. You will need one thermometer to detect the ambient or overall temperature of the room and the other, a handheld unit, to detect precise spots in the location being analyzed. The one for detecting the ambient air temperature can be a cheapy. Just a little palm-sized digital thermometer from Radio Shack or a car thermometer from the auto parts place down the street. The thermometer for detecting the actual cold spots should be more of an investment.

On some cable shows you may have seen some ghost hunters using IR non-contact digital thermometers to detect air temperature. Of course you have read my first book and know that was very silly of them. But, in case you haven't...

Thermometers, for the most part, have some sort of element in them that expands and contracts in relation to the temperature. Depending on the degree of expansion or contraction the thermometer can tell to what degree (greater or lesser) a substance such as air, water, chocolate, etc. is. An infrared thermometer does not measure temperature thru expansion or contraction. IR thermometers send out an invisible cone of infrared light. When the cone contacts another object it is reflected back and read by a sensor on the IR thermometer. The microprocessor inside IR thermometers covert the information gathered from the infrared radiation given off by the object into a temperature reading. Digital thermometers use electric resistance to measure temperature. A thermo-resistor reads the electric resistance of a substance such as air or water and sends that information to a computer or circuit to translate the information into a discernable temperature reading.

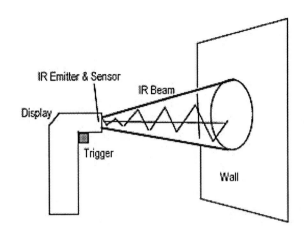

The basic IR thermometer (also known as a non-contact thermometer because it doesn't physically touch the object it's measuring) is composed of four visible parts --- the display screen for showing the readings, the infrared emitter for sending out the infrared beam, the sensor that receives the reflected infrared beam and the trigger that activates the beam. It's usually housed in a durable plastic casing in the better models or what resembles a McDonald's toy in others. There is a lens on the front where the IR beam is emitted. The trigger is usually spring loaded and recoils back when released. Some models have a fourth part --- a visible laser beam pointer. On some models, the laser pointer is activated by a separate switch, on others it goes off the same time the IR beam is fired. It is placed parallel to the IR emitter in the housing and the better-calibrated models will point dead center to where the IR beam is pointing. However, the visible laser and IR beam will veer off from one another the further the distance the IR thermometer is from the object is pointed at. This is irrelevant in most cases since if you are that far away you can't see the beam anyway. IR thermometers range in quality in most cases parallel to their price tag. They range in price from $40 to over $800.

So, how does an IR thermometer pick up temperatures anyway? Well, to know that we have to have a basic understanding of light; specifically infrared light.

Every object reflects, transmits and emits energy. Only emitted energy indicates the temperature of an object. When infrared thermometers measure an object's surface temperature they detect all three kinds of energy, therefore IR thermometers are adjusted to read only emitted energy. An IR thermometer will detect the temperature of fire. That is only because of the intense infrared heat. Errors can be caused by reflected light sources.

Distance to spot ratio refers to the distance from an object the IR thermometer is in relation to the size of the IR beam's cone. The spot is at the end of the cone. The resolution of the "spot" determines the accuracy of the device. The smaller the spot, the better the accuracy. Also, this means the further you are away from the object the less accurate the measurement. Another side effect is the further you are away from an object, the more likely you are to pick up the temperature of the area around the object. Particularly if the object being measured is relatively small. Boy, this is becoming an increasingly inaccurate piece of equipment!

The field-of-view refers to what was just mentioned. The closer you are, the better. If the light cone is larger than the object being measured, you will get an inaccurate reading.

So, to summarize, infrared thermometers detect the reflected light given off objects and determines the temperature of that object. IR thermometers have a high margin of error due to a number of factors. Reflections from light sources can create inaccurate readings. The distance from an object can adversely affect accuracy. The size of the object is also an important factor.

I guess you have gathered by now that IR thermometers are very bad at detecting air temperature and should not be used for that purpose. In fact, they are designed not to detect air temperature, only SOLID OBJECTS.

Digital Thermometers use electric resistance to measure temperature. A thermo-resistor reads the electric resistance (called the *Seebek Effect*) of a substance such as air or water and sends that information to a computer or circuit to translate the information into a discernable temperature reading. Nearly every thermo-resistor has a negative temperature coefficient which means their resistance decreases as the temperature increases. A multi-meter from Radio Shack (or the electronics supplier of your choice) can demonstrate this effect. Boiling water has a high resistance and reads 400 ohms at 100 degrees Celsius. A circuit in the digital thermometer does the math for you. Thermo-resistors take several seconds to get their info. The smaller the thermo-resistor, the faster the input will be. The smaller the thermo-resistor the more expensive it will be too. So, you got to pay more for faster service, just like in a French restaurant. C'est la vie.

Digital thermometers using thermo-coupler technology are much better for detecting air temperature since they actually detect air temperature. When you see that guy on cable shoot the IR thermometer at a wall and say there is a cold spot, either the ghost is coming through the wall and lowering the wall's temperature or he's reading the outdoor temperature through the window.

Map your area (be it a room or outdoor environment) using graph paper or the Room/Area Grid Forms from the Ghost Tech website (**www.ghosttech.net**). Then, walking very slowly in straight lines from one end of the room to another, take measurements of the room's temperature. Anything over 3 degrees should be documented. Best look for increases in temperature too and write that down.

The Weatherman's Friends Are Our Friends Too

One of the main reason ghost investigators use so many gadgets and gizmos are because we're all really nerds at heart. The other reason is because we believe that we are investigating one of mankind's greatest puzzles. By collecting enough data and sharing it with others we hope to piece together the secret that has eluded so many for so long.

Many believe that there may be a pattern to ghostly phenomena that will reveal the truth of the existence of ghosts. We just don't know yet what that pattern is. What are the conditions that must be present for a ghost to manifest? Why are ghosts in some places and not in others? These are the questions that justify the use of equipment that many ghost hunters share with the field of meteorology (the study of weather).

If the make-up of ghosts influence electrical and magnetic fields then likewise the make-up of that which influences electrical and magnetic fields may affect ghosts. Makes sense to me.

When water molecules form on objects, such as the case in humid locations, static electricity is less likely to occur. Dry locations are more likely to create static electrical charges. Which environment is best suited for ghosts? By sharing information collected from Hygrometers, perhaps we will find out one day.

Warm and cold temperature can affect air pressure. Air pressure can also affect human health. The pressure at 3,000 feet above sea level, such as in mountain towns, is lower than in a coastal city. Are ghosts affected by air temperature and pressure? Are places at higher altitudes more or less likely to be haunted than places at lower altitudes? Sharing information from Barometers and Altimeters may help with this question.

Violent explosions on the Sun's corona and chromosphere are as strong as tens of millions of H-bombs. These sunspots heat gases to millions of degrees and speed up electrons, protons and heavier ions to near the speed of light. Electromagnetic waves in all wavelengths of the electromagnetic spectrum are created and sent toward the Earth. The waves interfere with and occasionally damage or destroy electronics on Earth. Would these affect your readings in a haunted location? Would this affect ghosts? A visit to **www.spaceweather.com** may help you learn more. Documenting your findings will help everyone in the long run.

4. A STUDY OF HIGHER DIMENSIONS

"The key to growth is the introduction of higher dimensions of consciousness into our awareness."
- Lao Tzu (Chinese Taoist Philosopher, born in 600 BC)

Okay, I admit it! I hadn't read *Flatland: A Romance of Many Dimensions* in a long time when I wrote *Ghost Tech*. If you went out and bought a copy, or have read it yourself, you must realize that there are actually no humans at all in the book. I was trying to write about it from memory and was sure the three-dimensional character was a human being. It turns out he was just a sphere: Lord Sphere specifically. If you have no idea what I am talking about then you need to buy *Ghost Tech* now! Actually, in order to proceed with this chapter I will have to go over some stuff from *Ghost Tech*. Nevertheless, you should buy *Ghost Tech* regardless!

Anyway… in *Ghost Tech* I speculate that ghosts may use higher dimensions to do some of the things they do.

We live in a fourth dimensional universe --- height, width, length and time. You have height, width and length and travel forward through time. But, mathematics proves that there are other dimensions. There are levels of reality beyond our perception. Places with five, six even more than a dozen different dimensions! The problem is we cannot see these higher dimensions because our brains are hardwired for just four dimensions. However, there could be exceptions to the rule.

In 1854, a mathematician named Edwin A. Abbott wrote a book called *Flatland: A Romance of Many Dimensions*. In it, he describes what would happen if a two-dimensional character named A. Square met a three-dimensional being named Lord Sphere. A commentary on Victorian society, the book made some interesting observations on dimensional perceptions. In the story, Mr. Square meets a 3D sphere that tries to convince Mr. Square of the reality of fourth dimensional space. You see, Mr. A. Square lives on Flatland, a two dimensional world where only length and width exist, but no height. When the 3D Lord Sphere puts himself through Flatland to demonstrate his higher dimensions, Mr. Square sees Lord Sphere start as a point then become a series of small, then large and small again, circles that returns to a point and then disappear. Of course Mr. Square is horrified at this monster. By the end of story Mr. Square is convinced of the reality of three dimensions but still cannot visualize it.

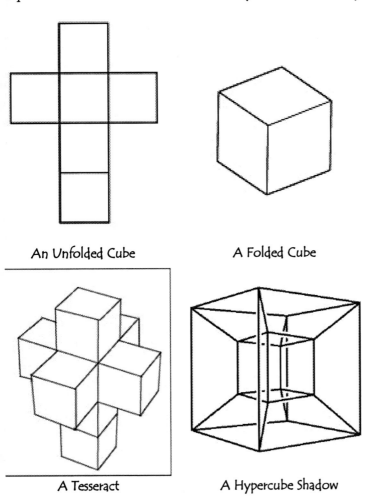

An Unfolded Cube

A Folded Cube

A Tesseract

A Hypercube Shadow

We, similarly, cannot visualize dimensions outside of our four because our brains are hardwired for four dimensions. If we unfold a cube into two dimensions it becomes a cross (see images). If we put the cross on Flatland, Mr. Square would perceive it as a twelve-sided shape. As we fold the cross "up" into a three-dimensional cube Mr. Square would see the cross disappear a section at a time until there was nothing but a square left in its place. A tesseract is essentially a three-dimensional cross. If we were to encounter a fifth dimensional being, they could fold the three-dimensional tesseract into a five-dimensional hypercube. We cannot visualize a hypercube with our limited 3D brains. However, with computer modeling we can see what light passed through a hypercube would look like and that is the shadow of a hypercube!

When we look down on Flatland we see everything at once --- all the people, houses, towns and roads. We even see inside the houses and inside the people! A fifth-dimensional person would be able to see inside us too.

They would see our front and back at the same time. A 5D man could see through and walk through walls just like a ghost! Fifth-dimensional people can also go anywhere they want instantly. Just like we can poke our finger through anyplace in Flatland, a 5D man could walk from New York to Tokyo instantly. To us, they would be virtually omnipotent.

Higher dimensions are inaccessible to those of us who are limited to just three dimensions of space. This fact can be demonstrated by an analogy proposed by mathematician and bigamist Charles Howard Hinton. The English mathematician was fascinated with the concept of higher dimensions. After being fired from Uppingham School in 1885, after having been arrested for bigamy, he packed up his stuff and one of his two wives and went to live in the land of the free. Too bad bigamy is bad here too. After a brief pause in his research into higher dimensions, when he invented the baseball-pitching machine, Hinton was able to return to his passion. When asked if we could ever access the realm of higher dimension, Hinton said that higher dimensions are too small for us to see.

> Most researchers believe that in the case of residual hauntings, a ghost walks through walls because the wall wasn't there when the spirit was alive. Since the ghost isn't conscience of its surroundings it does its decades old routine regardless of environmental changes. Higher dimensions may explain why interactive spirits can walk through walls.

Imagine a room full of smokers.... after a brief coughing fit, imagine the smoke curling off into the four corners of the room. The smoke will eventually travel to every inch of the room. When measuring this experiment in lung cancer, we can determine that the smoke has not exited into higher dimensions. Hinton suggested (as most scientists believe somewhat today) that higher dimensions exist at too small a level to be measured. They are smaller even than an atom. The energy requirement needed to access this incredibly small size is about a quadrillion times greater (yes, that's a real number, represented as a one followed by 24 zeros) than today's most powerful atom smasher. We literally have to bend time and space to do it. However, for anything already in a higher dimension, accessing lower dimensions is child's play.

Now, if you read Ghost Tech (or just this chapter) and were previously not versed in the theory of higher dimensions, then you may come away thinking that I was the first one to make the connection. You would be wrong.

The concepts behind our perspective of the universe in regard to dimensional perspective go back to about 370 B.C. Socrates talked about some weird stuff sometimes. No wonder he never wrote anything down! Luckily, Plato knew how to use a pen, or chisel, or whatever they used back then. Anyway, imagine some guys living in a cave underground. Now imagine those guys have been chained and restrained (see what I mean about weird!) since birth. They are restrained in such a way that they cannot move any part of there bodies and they were forced to look straight ahead at a wall. Behind them is a wall that is slightly inclined. Behind the wall is a light source that reflects the shadow of something on the inclined wall onto the cave wall in front of the men, like a Puppet Theater.

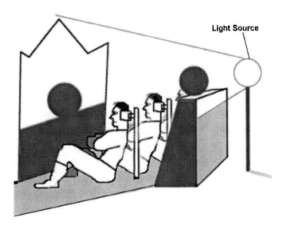

If there were an echo that bounced off the cave wall, then any voice spoken to them from behind them would appear to come from the shadows. If they were also able to converse with each other (but not see each other) then they would come to believe they were shadows themselves. Since these poor saps entire lives were spent in front of 2D shadows they would believe they were also 2D! What a deep, twisted philosopher Socrates was!

What if we were prisoners as well? What if our consciousness exists in a higher dimension but is restrained by the bonds of our physical 3D bodies? Since even before we were born, we have been chained to a three dimensional reality, never knowing anything else except three dimensions until we are released from bondage through death. Take that Socrates! I can philosophize too!

Yes, I know that some theologies have hinted at concepts like these for centuries now. In all myths and legends there are always some degree of truth, some higher truth in many cases. Perhaps this is another case in which earlier man could not quite comprehend this concept and developed a mystical explanation to accommodate ingrained and fundamental facts. Like I said, these are just theories.

Charles Hinton had names for the extra dimensions found beyond length, width and height. He called them "ana" and "kata". Just like a Flatlander cannot move "up" out of Flatland, you and I cannot move *ana* or *kata*. There could be a ghost just two feet *ana* and three feet *kata* from you right now! Although Plato and Socrates hinted at one's perspective in regards to higher dimensions it was a fellow philosopher named Henry More who associated higher dimensions with ghosts a little over 400 years ago.

More (coincidently a *Platonist*) believed that ghosts had more (pun intended) to them then just metaphysical conjectures. He believed that ghosts, and consequently your soul, occupy space like normal matter. G=M or GHOSTS equal MASS (I just made that up). But two pieces of matter cannot occupy the same place at the same time! That is, unless the extra mass rests in *hyperspace* (higher dimensional space), then it is not an issue at all. This suggests that your hyper-self (your soul/spirit/ghost/etc.) exists in hyperspace but is tethered in three-dimensional space by your body and mind. Like Socrates' cavemen, although you're part of a larger dimensional picture, you have no concepts outside of what your eyes perceive. When your 3D body dies your hyper-self would become un-tethered in this theory and "move on" so to speak.

It was German astronomy professor Johann Carl Friederich Zöllner from the University of Liepzig who really deservers credit for the introduction of ghosts into modern concepts of higher dimensions.

In 1875, Zöllner visited England to see cathode-ray tube inventor Sir William Crookes (actually Crookes wasn't knighted until 1897). This was at the time when Spiritualism was about to reach its peak. A lot of people believed in spiritualism, including Sherlock Holmes creator Sir Arthur Conan Doyle. Doyle believed in ghosts, fairies, magic and just about anything supernatural, a stark contrast to the ultra-skeptical detective Holmes.

Crookes was a bit of a conundrum in that he was a very serious, and probably boring, man of science and yet was really into spiritualism. He supported Henry Slade, an infamous medium from America. Slade was a self-proclaimed psychic who claimed to be able to contact ghosts from higher dimensions. In fact, Slade was a clever magician who used slight of hand tricks to fool the gullible. Would you believe that included some of the most prominent scientists who ever lived? Not just Crookes and Zöllner either but some who would go on to win the Nobel Prize, including the famous classical physicist Lord Raleigh.

Zöllner was convinced that Slade was in fact the "real deal". Using what many modern magicians would recognize as clever "magic tricks", Slade convinced Zöllner and many others that his "ghosts" could tie knots in rope that was sealed with wax at both ends, connect solid wooden rings together and affect objects in sealed jars. When in 1877 Slade was arrested on fraud charges, Zöllner shocked London society when he, and many other prominent scientists, came to Slade's defense. Slade was convicted anyway. Most were not surprised when Slade's friends from the fourth dimension didn't bust him out of jail.

Not Wormholes!

In Stephen Spielberg's paranormal film *Poltergeist*, journeys into higher dimensions are hinted at throughout the movie. In the movie, the little girl Carol Ann is apparently sucked (or pulled) out of our universe and into the "other side". A ball thrown in the bedroom lands in the living room. Would these be portals, as we know them today?

Many ghost hunters believe in a phenomenon called a *portal haunting*. Portal hauntings are places where there seems to be a nexus between our world and a mysterious "ghost zone" where the dead exist and other supernatural beings as well. These portals are used to explain hauntings at places where there is an unusual amount of ghostly happenings. Could ghosts be coming in through these in great numbers? Are these places a crossroads between worlds? Maybe. But they are not wormholes!

It would appear that too many ghost hunters are also *Star Trek* fans. This is not a bad thing until you start applying *Star Trek* science fiction to ghost hunting.

Wormholes are theoretical astronomical objects. When a star many times larger than our Sun dies it may explode and then collapse in on its self. There is only so much matter that can be in one place at one time and still have a stable gravitational pull. This is not one of those times. The matter present will collapse into an infinite density, a point in space where not even light can escape its gravitational pull. This is called a *black hole*. We know they exist because they have been observed by modern radio telescopes. Some scientists think they may exit into another universe or connect places in this universe or even places in other times. They call these theoretical objects wormholes.

Recently, I came across a website that hinted that portals are wormholes. I guess that is logical conclusion. I mean they are both supposed to be entrances to other places, right?

Well, yes, except for two blaring differences: radiation and extreme pressure. If you were a ghost hunting at a cemetery and a wormhole opened up you and your team would be bombarded with radiation in the form of high energy x-rays. Then, if you lived long enough to get a little closer you would be burned up from the heat and then torn to pieces from the intense forces present. Maybe that's not a problem for Jean-Luc Picard, but I think it may be for you and your team.

A Note on New Research!

Can you imagine what it would be like if some mad-scientist tried to create a black hole here on Earth? You would probably envision the device imploding in on itself then collapsing as everything in the lab is sucked into the depths of the black hole's infinite density. Then, at nearly the speed of light, the singularity (the black holes "point of no return") would smash through the floor and then journey to the center of Earth's gravity --- the core! It may pendulum back and fourth a bit before settling in the center and then begin "eating" the planet from the inside out. Eventually, all of the Earth and everything in it will be pulled into oblivion and then, with no place else to go, the ultimate form of destruction in the universe would head to our sun and slowly blink it out of existence...

Well, guess what, researchers (10,000 scientists from 50 counties) are building a 17 mile particle accelerator in Geneva, Switzerland for the purpose of creating their own black hole! Crazy you say? Well, you don't have to worry about the end of the world. They are only making miniature black holes.

Tiny black holes would not last long enough to pull in any matter. They would flash out of existence before causing any damage.

Theoretically....

In reality, larger collisions of particles than what can be created in the new particle accelerator already happen in Earth's atmosphere when it is struck by cosmic rays from space. So, there could be black holes being created and vanishing right above us all the time, but only if other dimensions actually exist.

In the particle accelerator, two protons will be fired at each other at close the speed of light. If extra dimensions actually exist, they will appear to increase the force of gravity in the proximity of the collision. The force of gravity will increase at this point until smaller particles called *quarks* (pronounced like "cork") join together. The joining will collapse space and time and create a really, really tiny black hole. The black hole will be smaller than the nucleus of an atom --- tens of thousands of times smaller. The black hole will last only a microsecond before it dissolves into a dozen different kinds of particles called Hawking radiation. If this works than higher dimensions will virtually be proven to exist. We'll all find out in 2007 when the experiment is put to the test.

5. UNDEAD CATS!

"Those who are not shocked when they first come across quantum theory cannot possibly have understood it."
- Niels Bohr on Quantum Physics

"God does not play dice with the universe."
- Albert Einstein on Quantum Physics

"Einstein, don't tell God what to do."
- Niels Bohr in response to Einstein

"If you want to exist in this universe, you have to obey its rules."
I cannot count how many times I have said that in conversation, at lectures and in my books. I try to stress how fundamental a rule this is. It is very important to the structure of the universe and reality that this rule never be broken. Whatever ghosts are doesn't matter. For them (ghosts) to exist they must and will affect the environment in some way.

"But how do know this is true Vince," you might ask.

Well, that's what this chapter is about. If you bought this book (good call!) then you are probably already sure that ghosts have a place in scientific research. At least you have a pretty good idea. Some of those who believe in ghosts might argue that ghosts are "ethereal" and "supernatural" and have no place in science. They would say that I am wasting my time with trying to collect theories of their existence since they can neither be proven nor disproved. Ghosts are magic some people argue. If they don't want you too, you will never detect them.

If ghosts are magic and they don't want you to detect them then that would mean when you die you develop "ghost powers"! Upon your demise as a living being you suddenly become aware of magical ghost powers. You can levitate objects with your ghostly mind. You can pass through walls since you are a ghost and you know it! You are Casper and Slimer rolled into one. You also have a mission! Now, as a ghost, your job is to scare people out of your house. Kind of like the poor couple in the movie *Beetlejuice*. Maybe you'll even have an instruction book on how to act like a proper spook. You'll have detailed instructions on the correct way to rattle chains and techniques for getting just the right BOO!

Modern day ghost hunters use scientific instrumentation to try and detect the presence of ghosts. They use EMF meters, digital thermometers and the like to try to see if ghosts are in the room with them or maybe out in a field or cemetery. Not to sound like a broken record, but they do not use them to detect ghosts directly. Once again --- we are not the *Ghostbusters!* We do not have devices that work like PKE meters like Egon and Ray had. I wish we did, it make our job so much easier.

Now, the title of this chapter is *Undead Cats*, which makes it seem like something written by friend and colleague Rosemary Ellen Guiley (who wrote the *Encyclopedia of Vampires, Werewolves, and Other Monsters*). But no, this chapter is not about zombie, vampire or were-cats. The chapter title is derived from a thought experiment dreamed up by one Erwin Schrödinger who was trying to debunk the Heisenberg Uncertainty Principle. He ended up contributing to it instead. Whoa! I'm getting ahead of myself now. There's some splainin' to do here, Lucy! When I am done explaining I hope you will understand a little better why everything that exists must obey the laws of the universe!

Now, pay attention. What we are about to go into befuddled Einstein all the way until his death in 1955 at the age of 76.

Science's Uncertain Principles

As I mentioned earlier, this is a very complicated subject. However, do not let that keep you from reading on. I will not be going into too much of the history of subject of quantum mechanics. That information could easily fit into its own book and in fact already has (read the excellent *In Search of Schrodinger's Cat: Quantum Physics and Reality* by John Gribbin for more on that). I really think your smart enough anyway since you bought this book in the first place.

Earlier in this book we mentioned how we take it for granted that meteorites exist and have created some really big craters here on Earth. It's funny now thinking about how only a few decades ago many scientists weren't sure if meteorite craters were caused by rocks from space or extinct volcanoes. Many things that we take for granted as simply existing were not so easily accepted not too long ago. The concept of atoms, for example, existed as early as ancient Greece. We now accept atoms as a fact of life and take them for granted. However, it wasn't' until the early 20th century that the scientific community started taking it seriously.

As early as 370 B.C., Democritus of Abdera suggested that all things could be broken down into smaller pieces until eventually you got to an unchangeable object called an atom. "The only existing things are atoms and empty space; all else is opinion," he said. However, the more romantic concept of four "elements" of air, earth, fire and water proposed by good ole Aristotle remained the more popular theory for centuries.

Seventeenth century English chemist Robert Boyle liked the idea of atoms and so did Sir Isaac Newton.

Newton on atoms and their history:

Atomism arose as an explanatory scheme with the ancient Greeks (around 400BC), Leucippus and Democritus, and Epicurus, and the Roman poet, Lucretius. At the most fundamental level atomism is the belief that all phenomena are explicable in terms of the properties and behaviour of ultimate, elementary, localized entities (or 'fundamental particles'). Thus it prescribes a strategy for the construction of scientific theories in which the behaviour of complex bodies is to be explained in terms of their component parts. That strategy has led to many of the successes of modern physical science, though these do not prove that there actually are 'ultimate entities' of the type postulated by atomism.

Their (the atomists) analysis goes 'behind' the appearance of minute, unchangeable and indestructible 'atoms' separated by the emptiness of 'the void'. It is the void which is said to make change and movement possible. All apparent change is simply the result of rearrangements of the atoms as a consequence of collisions between them. This seems to lead to mechanical determinism, though, in an attempt to leave room for freewill, Epicurus and Lucretius postulated that atoms might 'deviate' in their courses.

However if 'what exists' is 'atoms', what of the 'void'? In different ways both Aristotle and Descartes denied that there could be such a thing as literally 'empty space'. Physically therefore they saw the world as a plenum. Atomism was also associated with atheism, since as Lucretius put it, 'Nothing can ever be created out of nothing, even by divine power.' Conversely no thing can ever become nothing – so the atomists proposed a strict principle of conservation of matter.

The attempt of the ancient atomists to solve a metaphysical problem about the nature of change resulted in a brilliantly fruitful strategy for the construction of theories in the physical sciences. However there are unanswered philosophical objections to atomism and the very successes it has stimulated suggest that 'the stuff of the world' cannot ultimately be understood in terms of atomism. A thoroughgoing positivism will continue to hold that 'atomic theories' are simply devices for talking about observable phenomena.

(The Concise Encyclopedia of Western Philosophy and Philosophers, 1991)

It wasn't until the early 19th century that a color-blind fellow named Charles Dalton put atoms on the map. It was Dalton, a British chemist and physicist, who gave atoms many of the characteristics that high school kids learn and quickly forget today. One thing he got wrong though was that atoms are indivisible. Can you say atomic bomb? I knew you could...

It was a relatively (pun intended) short time later that Albert Einstein proved the existence of atoms once and for all in 1905. His paper on the photoelectric effect demonstrated the emission of electrons from a material as a result of light striking its surface, something that could only be proven with atoms. Einstein would later win the Nobel Prize in 1921 for this work.

New Zealand born Ernest Rutherford developed a theory in regards to

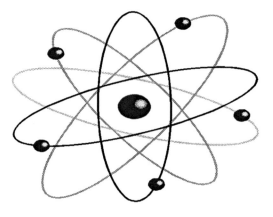

the structure of atoms in 1911. Unlike the image of a nucleus surrounded by spinning electrons, akin to moons rapidly orbiting a weird planet, like we were taught in school, the atomic structure is a bit different in reality. Rutherford (who invented the first EMF detector in 1897!) showed that the atom is more like a nucleus surrounded by an electron "cloud". Although most of the atom is empty space (Imagine the period at the end of this sentence is a nucleus of an atom. If you placed the nucleus on the torch of the Statue of Liberty, the circling cloud of electrons would be no closer than the bottom of the base 306' 8" below. The nucleus by the way is 100,000 times smaller than the atom itself) an electric charge, protons and neutrons keep the electrons from falling into the nucleus and also keeps other atoms from (under normal conditions) interacting.

Nucleus

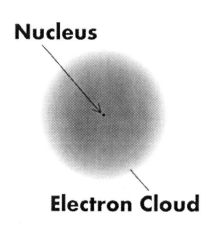

Electron Cloud

Just to round things out, it was British physicist (there are a lot of British and German scientists in this book aren't there?) Sir Joseph John Thomson who discovered that cathode rays are composed of negatively charged particles called electrons. Ernest Rutherford would discover the proton in 1919 and predict the existence of the neutron. Rutherford's colleague James Chadwick (also a Limey) would discover the neutron in 1932.

"So what's the point Vince?"

The point is I think some of the readers possibly need a little set up to refresh their memories in regard to the nature of atoms and the subatomic world in general. Now we're getting into the really weird stuff!

The most amazing principle, one that has stayed experiment after experiment, of quantum theory is the Heisenberg Uncertainty Principle. It is the genie in the bottle. It is Pandora's box. It is... Some other metaphor I can't think of right now. The Heisenberg Uncertainty Principle clearly states that you cannot measure the position and velocity of a subatomic particle at the same time. If you measure its speed, you change its position. Measure its position and you change its velocity. Amazing, huh? Ok, let me elaborate since the implications may not be obvious at first.

The Global Positioning System, or GPS, is an amazing bit of technology. Using multiple government satellites orbiting the earth, pocket-sized devices can calculate the latitude, longitude and even altitude of a moving object within a few feet. Astronomers can calculate the position of planets and other heavenly bodies so precisely we can land a robot on Mars millions of miles away or send a probe to a comet while it's moving at thousands of miles an hour through our solar system. But no scientist anywhere can predict the speed and position of a little ole electron with absolute certainty. This is the part that made Einstein say, "God does not play dice with the Universe." Why can we not measure a subatomic particle's speed and position? Well, because electrons, protons and the rest of the subatomic particles are really, really small of course.

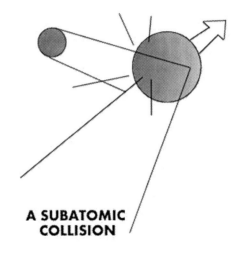

A SUBATOMIC COLLISION

So, how does one even try to measure the speed or position of, lets say, an electron? Unfortunately you will need to shoot another electron or photon or some other subatomic particle at it. There are things smaller than electrons but nothing smaller can be measured. And even then we will have to shoot something at it that will no doubt alter its direction and/or speed. Since rulers and gauges are made of atoms and we cannot make a measuring device small enough to measure an electron so we look at the reactions that are created by shooting other particles at it.

German born Werner Heisenberg will always be associated with the theory of quantum mechanics due to his famous *principle of uncertainty*. The Uncertainty Principle is an elaboration on the fact that attempting to measure a subatomic particle's velocity <u>and</u> position is impossible. The concept was, and is, extremely controversial. Many scientists had some major issues with this concept. People of science like to believe that everything and anything is measurable. Scientists once thought that is you could measure the speed and position of every particle in the universe you could know everything that was and could be. It was believed that one-day building sized computers would predict the weather. So much for that! Some scientists thought that Heisenberg's theory was a challenge to the scientific community. Papers were regularly being published that contained "thought experiments" trying to prove Heisenberg wrong. Even Einstein got into the fray. However, the most famous thought experiment proposed to discredit the uncertainty principle in fact only proved how weird the reality of it really was.

Dead Or Alive?

Austrian scientist Erwin Schrödinger tried to show how silly a concept quantum mechanics was. No one thought to tell him how silly a first name Erwin is.

In case you haven't picked it up yet, nothing is real, according to quantum mechanics, which is not observed. Besides the inability to measure the momentum and position of subatomic particles, the other revelation of the uncertainty principle was the effect of consciousness on reality. See... I told you it would get weird!

The effect of human consciousness on reality becomes evident when you use a quantum event (subatomic-sized interactions) to determine the outcome of macroscopic events (people-sized interactions). This is where Schrödinger's "cat in a box" experiment comes into play.

Imagine --- if you will, a cat in a box,
Secure on all sides with four silver locks.

Every side of the box is completely opaque.
Nor could you hear what's inside for the experiment's sake.

Whoa! The ghost of Dr. Seuss momentarily possessed me! Um, so anyway... also inside the box is a vial of poison placed beneath a delicately balanced hammer. The hammer is connected to mechanism that is connected to a Geiger counter. The Geiger counter is right above a radioactive element with a 50/50 percent chance of decaying within a certain time period. If the Geiger counter detects the decay it will activate the mechanism that will drop the hammer and smash the vial of poison. If it doesn't detect the decay, Morris will live to father more kittens. Also, PETA might be more lenient on your lawsuit.

Now, it gets really weird. In order to find out what happened to poor Morris, we have to open the box. But before we open the box we can speculate. All the apparatus was internal. We cannot see the hammer, vial or cat. It was sound-proofed too, so we couldn't hear the vial breaking or Morris' last "meow" or sigh of relief. However, Morris was able to breath thanks to a previously unmentioned oxygen supply, so we cannot suppose he asphyxiated. So, what do we speculate about our unfortunate (either way, he's part of an awfully nasty lab experiment) feline friend?

Dead... Or Alive?

How about ---- both! Until we open that box Morris exists in a flux of existence. He is both dead and alive at the same time! No, I do not mean "the kitty that walks at midnight". He exists in two realities simultaneously until someone opens the box. In one reality, he will once again know the joy of toy mice and kitty litter and in the other reality, well --- he is litter.

Only by opening the box can you force one reality to take precedent over the other --- through conscience observation! Schrödinger himself thought this was ridiculous, but repeated experiments over the years have shown the theory to be quite solid. Quantum theory shows that every object exists in all possible states until the object is measured or simply observed. The moon has Jackie Gleason's face on it until you look up and prove it does not --- so far, so good on that one.

Another implication of these facts is that you cannot measure or observe anything without changing it. Not just sub-atomic particles --- anything!

When the Crocodile Hunter peeps over some mosquito infested swamp grass to get a better view of a 12-foot croc rising from beneath the water to eat some goofy Australian (not to say all Australians are goofy, just this one) he, the Croc Hunter, has changed the environment.

Photons enter your eye and are reflected off the retina back into the environment, which influence other photons and other particles that would not have otherwise been influenced by your presence, you trouble-maker! Your warm breath will excite the molecules in the air and increase the air temperature. Your bad breath (have a Tic-Tac)

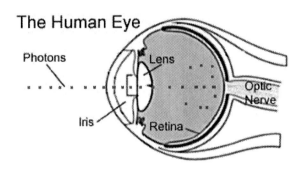

The Human Eye

Photons

Lens

Iris

Retina

Optic Nerve

will draw mosquitoes to the carbon dioxide you exhale if you are outside in the warmer months of the year. Oh, and of course you will be consciously forcing the outcome of different states of reality by your mere presence.

Theoretically, such small changes can cause large-scale changes to occur. This is the nature of *Chaos Theory*. It has been speculated that a butterfly in China can flap its wings and cause a hurricane in the Gulf of Mexico (that's why you should always buy American --- even butterflies in other countries don't like us). This is called the *Butterfly Effect* (no, I didn't just make that up and it is not just the name of a really bad time travel movie). In one of science's more holistic aspects it states, for the most part, everything influences everything else.

So you see --- if you want to exist in the universe you have to obey its rules. No matter what a ghost is it will influence the environment in some way.

That's life, so to speak...

6. THE SENSITIVE SIDE OF GHOST HUNTING

"Here's something to think about: How come you never see a head-line like 'Psychic Wins Lottery'?"
-Jay Leno

I was at a local, Civil War era battlefield for a weekend of ghost hunt-ing with some friends and colleagues not too long before I began writing this book. At our base site, I was critiquing an author of one of the many ghost-hunting books out there. Specifically, I was criticizing his sugges-tions for using devices that add extra elements into the environment (I touch on this more in *Ghost Tech,* by the way) such as Van De Graff gen-erators and negative ion emitters. Little did I know that the group "psy-chic" was listening in on me. Little did I also know that she/he was a big fan of the author I was not a big fan of, if only for the bits on using devices like Van De Graff generators.

Now, don't get me wrong, I believe there are people out there who are more sensitive to ghosts, hauntings and other paranormal phenomena than the average citizen. We like to call them "sensitives" as apposed to "psychics" due to the negative associations there are with the word "psy-chic". Although I have said that on a psychic scale from one to ten I would read negative five, I know there are people out there that are more apt to "feel" ghosts than I am to take a picture of one. I myself have used sensi-tives on investigations many times in the past and will continue to do so.

Kelly Weaver from Pennsylvania is someone whose abilities I have absolute faith in. I have worked with her in the past. In fact, this chapter is all about explaining some of the theories behind how there can be those who are more sensitive than most. Before we can talk about the "real deal" thouugh, lets go back to my Civil War battlefield psychic adventure story.

Generally when I have met what I consider an authentic sensitive, they are shy about discussing (except for Kelly --- there is an exception for every rule) their abilities. The very flamboyant mediums and psychics are the ones I have learned to scrutinize a little harder. Although I said noth-ing of my doubts about her/his "powers", I believe she/he picked up my skepticism just the same. I don't think they "psychically" detected my disbelief in their paranormally enhanced insight into the haunted battle-fields of the area, I just think I was bad at hiding it. I began to "detect" that they didn't like me.

When we got out onto the battlefield, we were investigating a site where there had been a barn that was burned down during the battle that took place there. To the best of the knowledge of the Civil War history experts present (and that knowledge was formidable, I can assure you) this was perhaps the first time a ghost hunt had been done here. Immediately upon setting up, the "psychic" began talking about how the soldiers felt and what some of their names were.

I began to set up an *enticement experiment*. An enticement experiment uses objects from different time periods (money, toys, antiques, etc.) or reenacting events from the past (playing poker in a haunted casino or shouting a roll call in a battlefield for example) to "entice" reactions from ghosts. I placed reproduction Confederate and Union paper money and coins around the site to see if ghosts are as greedy in death as they are in life. Even the most honorable soldier wouldn't pass up the chance to get free cash, right? I mean, if someone's just leaving it around... Anyway, when I walked back to check on the experiment and to take some pictures, a friend and colleague who lingered near our medium friend over-heard them say some interesting things about my experiment.

Actually they were "quoting" the ghosts, who had some interesting things to say about my experiment. "Why is he leaving the money", the medium said the ghosts said. "Does he think we're thieves?"

Of course, the "psychic" didn't repeat this stuff when I was near. They just began to hyperventilate from all of the "energy" in the air. Then they started to get attacked by mosquitoes (remember what I said earlier about mosquitoes being attracted to exhaled carbon monoxide?). Shortly after our clairvoyant became dinner to several dozen mosquitoes, "Nostradamus" started spouting off about the ghosts saying, "We had to go".

What a coincidence! The rest of us who were not as annoyed by the mosquitoes (nor as annoying in general) and who had the "sense" to put on bug repellent, didn't detect this message at all ourselves. Eat your heart out Uri Geller!

Now I am not necessarily saying that this person is totally devoid of "psychic ability". I'll leave that up to the reader.

A Retro-Cognitive Look into the History of Psychical Research

In my first book I mentioned what was perhaps the oldest recorded experiment in parapsychology.

It was about 550 B.C. that the first recorded paranormal experiment took place. King Croesus of Lydia, according to Greek historian Herodotus, wanted to know if he should attack Persia. So, he sent seven messengers to the seven top oracles of the day. He told the messengers to wait one hundred days after they left and ask each oracle what the king was doing that day. The king was making a big bronze kettle full of turtle and lamb soup a la Croesus. Well, five oracles got it wrong, one was almost right but only the Oracle of Delphi was dead on.

I count the grains of sand on the ocean shore
I measure the ocean's depths
I hear the dumb man
I likewise hear the man who keeps silence.
My senses perceive an odor as when one cooks
Together the flesh of the tortoise and the lamb,
Brass is on the sides and beneath,
Brass also covers the top.

With the Delphi Oracle's clairvoyant accuracy assured the king asked if he should go to war. The Oracle replied, "...An empire will be lost that day." The king went to war, sure of his victory. To bad it was Croesus' empire that was lost. Doh!

Parapsychology is the scientific study of psychic and/or paranormal phenomena. Psychologist and philosopher Max Dessoir probably coined the term parapsychology some time in the 1880s. Although many who study the phenomena of ghosts and hauntings call themselves parapsychologists (don't forget Ray, Egon and Peter!) the science was originally meant only to study the psychical such as ESP and telekinesis. Ghosts went in and out and back into the picture a little later. Bigfoot, E.T. and the Loch Ness Monster belong to the fields of crypto-zoology and exobiology.

Clairvoyance (the so-called "sixth-sense") appears throughout the ages and even in the bible (the Witch of Endor, for example, was a practitioner of necromancy, or the art of talking to the deceased). Joseph Glanvill studied weird manifestations, which we would call "poltergeist phenomena" now and wrote about it in 1681. Prospero Lambertini (who would become Pope Benedict XIV) was a Vatican sanctioned miracle investigator in the mid-1700s. University of Vienna student Anton Mesmer developed concepts dealing with, what he called, "animal magnetism". His research into the mind led to developments in hypnotism (Mesmer lends his name to "mesmerism"). His animal magnetism concept and belief in the healing powers of "magnetized water" got him trouble with the law while in Paris. Ben Franklin and other scientists of the time saw to that.

Parapsychology really took off as a science and received its name in the mid to late 19th century. This was during the rise of the pseudo-religion known as "Spiritualism". This frustrated many scientists of the day since it was widely believed that all that metaphysical nonsense was on its way out with advent of more logical scientific advances such as electric light bulbs, telegraphs and the theory of evolution. Many feel that Spiritualism truly began with the Fox Sisters and their talking with spirits by means of rapping. No, they weren't also the precursors to Snoop Dog, they would tap on tables and supposedly the ghosts would tap back.

It all began in 1848, when strange "thumping" noises were heard throughout the Fox household. Maggie, Kate and Leah Fox were living in Rochester, New York with their parents. Margaret Fox, the girl's mother, thought the noises were from ghosts. In March of that year the girls noticed that when they clapped their hands, the noises or "rapping" would answer back. They developed a complex tapping/clapping way of communication. The "ghost" told the sisters that he was a street peddler who had been murdered by a former occupant of the house they now lived in. Amazingly, human teeth, hair and bones were found buried in the cellar!

When the media of the time (easily as sensationalized as today) got wind of it Leah, the oldest sister at 34 (Maggie was 15 and Kate was 12), assumed the position of manager and publicist. Their "act" would make the Fox Sisters world famous. Ka-ching!

Spiritualism was on the move and even the White House wasn't impervious against the invasion! First Lady Mary Todd Lincoln held séances on a regular basis in the president's home. Mediums were popping up on every corner faster than you can say "ectoplasm". No doubt the most famous of these mediums was D.D. Home.

Daniel Douglas Home (like so many celebrities today, his name was pronounced differently than you would think --- it was pronounced 'Hume'). This Scottish psychic could levitate himself over the heads of onlookers; move objects with his mind, change the shape and size of his body and was even fireproof! David Blaine has nothing on this guy! It was believed that Home inherited his "powers" from his mother. Home's family moved to America in 1842 when he was nine to live with his aunt, Mary Cook. She later kicked him out for what she thought were incarnations of the Devil despite protests from clergy who thought he was a "gift from God".

Ten years later Home would accomplish his greatest feat: levitation! At a séance being conducted in wealthy businessman Ward Cheney's Connecticut home the medium known as D.D. Home flew to the ceiling of the room in front of a skeptical reporter and an astonished Ward. The reporter would write:

Suddenly, without any expectation of the part of the company, Home was taken up into the air. I had hold of his hand at the time and I felt his feet - they were lifted a foot from the floor. He palpitated from head to foot with the contending emotions of joy and fear, which choked his utterances. Again and again, he was taken from the floor, and the third time he was taken to the ceiling of the apartment, with which his hands and feet came into gentle contact.

Home would spend most of his life without a home of his own. He preferred to live in the homes of the rich and upper class. He never charged for his performances though. He would later marry and sire a son and travel in retirement until his death in 1886 from tuberculosis. To this day, no one has effectively explained Home's feats of the supernatural. His levitations were done in private homes where he could not have rigged any sort of effective ropes and pulley system. Nor can anyone explain some of his other abilities. Today D.D. Home remains a mystery. But other mediums of the time were not so lucky as to remain as historic "mysteries"...

There is little doubt that the vast majority of mediums and clairvoyants of the time were frauds. Many people were conned out of fortunes while mediums became rich. Who were fakes and who were legitimate psychics? Several people, and newly founded agencies, would answer the call for clarification and, mostly, legitimate research.

London scholars Henry Sidgwick, Sir William F. Barret and Frederic W.H. Myers (who would coin the term "telepathy") would form, with others, the Society for Psychical Research (SPR) in 1882. In 1885, several American scholars would form the American Society for Psychical Research (ASPR) in Boston. These organizations would perform the first controlled experiments into the paranormal. Also on the rise were the first really "hardcore" skeptics, such as Harry Houdini, who debunked many a fraud, but still believed in "something", and "nutty" "true believers", like Sir Arthur Conan Doyle who believed in "fairies".

By the 1880s, interest in spiritualism began to wane. In 1888, Maggie and Kate Fox made an appearance in New York where they admitted to faking everything.

Smear campaigns, scandal and fraud would tarnish the reputations of the members of SPR and the ASPR for the first few years of their existence. However, the groups would weather the controversies fairly well and establish themselves as leaders in paranormal research, a reputation that remains until this day. Now, if you are at all familiar with any of this history so far you are no doubt waiting for the bit on famous ghost researcher Harry Price. Well, sorry to disappoint you but I am going to skip that bit. I already covered Mr. Price in *Ghost Tech* and Troy Taylor has extensively covered Price in a few of his books. Besides, this chapter is about parapsychology and sensitives and although Harry Price did investigate a few mediums in his day, he's better known as a ghost researcher.

So, out with metaphysics and in with PKE and science! We now leap forward in the chronology of psychical research to the 1930s, where research into parapsychology really began, thanks to Dr. J.B Rhine.

Joseph Banks Rhine was born in a Pennsylvania log cabin in 1895. His

father was a skeptic of all the stories of ghosts and magic that are prevalent in small Pennsylvanian mountain towns. Despite that, Rhine would develop an acute curiosity for the paranormal that would last the rest of his life. Although he felt he had a true religious experience at the age of 12, when he met Louisa Ella Weckesser, a skeptic of religion, he would give up thoughts of a career in ministry for his future wife.

Rhine would also give up a career in forestry for paranormal research after hearing a lecture by none other than Sir Arthur Conan Doyle in 1922 Chicago. Rhine's first Ph. D. was in botany after all.

Rhine joined ASPR in 1924 and began working for ASPR's *Journal.* It was with the *Journal* that Rhine began reading stories about Boston medium "Margery" who's real name was Mina Stinson Crandon. Crandon is mainly to fault for a major upheaval of APSR that resulted in the organization's split, which in turn resulted in the formation of a rival group called the Boston Society for Psychical Research (which, by the way, shares the same acronym as my own group the Baltimore Society for Paranormal Research or BSPR). Although there is much in the way of evidence to suggest that Crandon had some psychic ability, there were also many reasons to suggest part of her séances were fraudulent. After meeting with Crandon and seeing her manipulate objects with her feet and hands in the dark, Rhine resigned from ASPR due to their unwavering support for such an obvious fraud.

Walter Franklin Prince, an Episcopal Minister and psychical researcher, was originally a member of ASPR, who also became disillusioned due to ASPR's support of Crandon. He resigned from ASPR as well and moved to Boston to take a position with the Boston Society for Psychical Research. Prince introduced the Rhine's to Detroit school administrator, John F. Thomas, who would later be the first person to receive a Ph. D. in Parapsychology from a school in the United States. The Rhine's, along with Thomas, left for Duke University to study under psychologist William McDougall. McDougall, who was originally from Lancashire, England, was president of SPR in England and became president of ASPR after accepting a job at Harvard in 1920. After trying to create a better set of standards at APSR, he was later rejected and replaced. It was then that McDougall accepted a position at Duke.

Rhine began as Thomas' and McDougall's research assistant. After Thomas received his Ph. D. in Parapsychology, Rhine became a professor of Psychology at Duke. It was around this time that Rhine began his famous ESP card tests. Rhine's research began taking up so much space that a separate lab was created called the Parapsychology Laboratory or the Department of Parapsychology. Just before Rhine retired in 1962, he estab-

lished the Foundation for Research on the Nature of Man (FRNM). The University's Parapsychology Laboratory moved to FRNM in 1965. J.B Rhine would pass away in 1980, fifteen years before the centennial of his birth, when FRNM would be renamed the Rhine Research Center in his memory.

Rhine had divided ESP into three categories. They were:

1.   *Clairvoyance* - the ability to acquire information directly from the environment.

2.   *Telepathy* - the ability to read minds or communication with others through mind-to-mind contact.

3. *Precognition* - the ability to predict future events and outcomes.

Another, fourth form of ESP was later devised after a visitor to Duke University's Department of Parapsychology bragged that he could make dice land where he wanted. I'd love to take that guy to Atlantic City with me! This fourth type was called *psychokinesis* or *PK*. A new emphasis on statistics would be made that would carry on to this day.

What is Psi?

As I have mentioned before, we have used sensitives in investigations in the past. These are people that I have learned to trust and believe in and some of whom I call friends. I couldn't tell you their names though. Not because I don't remember them (some friend!) but because they chose to remain anonymous. Most true sensitives do. It's the flamboyant "I feel the soul of U.S. Grant" psychics that I have trouble believing. Not that all public "out of the closet" psychics aren't genuine; it's just that I have seen too many people taken advantage of by charlatans. Most of the sensitives I have come in contact with that seem to exhibit real paranormal abilities are not that open to discussing them. So, assuming that the sensitives I believe are actually gifted with something akin to ESP are real, how is that possible?

It is well-known in the medical community that some people evidently exhibit an evident over-sensitivity to electricity and electromagnetic fields (EMF). This is sometimes called *electric hypersensitivity*. Due to the risk of creating paranormal hypochondriacs, I am going to tell the readers that no doctor will diagnose you with *electric hypersensitivity* since there is not nearly enough information available on it and certainly not enough funding. Why some people are electrically hypersensitive is still unknown.

Those who apparently have electric hypersensitivity will get sick when in close proximity to cell phone towers, power lines, fuse and circuit breaker power boxes, CRT monitors, etc. Victims may succumb to dermatological problems such as dry and itchy skin. Other problems include dizziness, fatigue, headache, difficulties in concentration, memory problems, anxiety, depression, etc., respiratory problems (difficult breathing), gastrointestinal symptoms, eye and vision symptoms, palpitations, and so on. As someone who is around electronics all the time, I couldn't imagine having an illness that would make me sick to be near my wonderful gadgets! Gasp!

A few of the sensitives I have met have exhibited symptoms of electric hypersensitivity. They do indeed get sick and/or uncomfortable around strong electrical and electromagnetic fields. At a location the Baltimore Society for Paranormal Research investigated in the summer of 2004, the sensitive on the team had headaches and dizzy spells every time we walked through a certain area between the kitchen and the living room. There was no way this person could have known this, but there was a large number of power lines and boxes on the wall outside supplying the apartment complex we were conducting the investigation at. We didn't find out until we started using our EMF meters and then we began picking up the unusual fields present in that area. Also, the power lines were in the back of complex and we came in the front. None of the investigative team had been there before that night.

Is it possible that some people may be more susceptible to ghosts and hauntings in the same way that some people are susceptible to EMF and electrical fields? Perhaps sensitives are like antennas for memory possessions. Due to their hypersensitivity they can pick up the electromagnetic resonance of events from the past. This is, of course, just another theory.

Psi doesn't just involve the ability to see and feel ghosts. Many parapsychologists don't even study or acknowledge this aspect of ESP. What they do study is the before mentioned: clairvoyance - the ability to acquire information directly from the environment; telepathy - the ability to read minds or communication with others through mind-to-mind contact; and precognition - the ability to predict future events and outcomes. If we are really going to try to understand how some people are able to communicate with ghosts to the degree that they can reveal unknown (at least to the sensitive in question) information about the past (or retrocognition without the help of ghosts) and/or location being investigated then we should really look into these other aspects of *Extra-Sensory Perception.*

So, forget about the movie *Scanners.* Super-powerful psychics in real life have exploded no heads, at least as far as I know. However, clairvoyance has been studied and researched enough to suggest that many things are possible. The word *clairvoyance* comes from the French "clear seeing". It is sometimes called the "second sight". It is the ability to see things as they happen from a distance and without Superman's telescopic and x-ray vision. Remember the Time-Life Books commercials in the '80's for *Mysteries of the Unknown?* There was one where the narrator describes a woman who feels a sharp pain in her hand and hundreds of miles away her daughter burns her hand. Coincidence? I think not.

Was the mother of the burn victim feeling the sensation of her daughter's burn or was she reading her mind? Some parapsychologists do not differentiate between what is clairvoyance and telepathy (the ability to read minds). They prefer the term General ESP or GESP. So how can either be possible anyway? Perhaps they are subconsciously really good at chess? Well, chess as metaphor anyway. To know the rules of chess is not enough to be good at it. You have to be able to predict your opponent's next move. Some excellent chess players can predict an opponent's next few moves - --- sometimes as many as ten moves in advance or more! Is it possible that that some people are subconsciously putting together the outcome of events? Sometimes they get the information at the same time as an event happens and sometimes before. For every possible outcome that occurs in their lives they are able to predict the outcome of every 50/50 chance. But there are other possibilities.

With that we come to precognition. Many have heard the report of the parapsychologist who was always on time for his appointments. He always rushed to get to the airport and always made sure everything was ready in advance. Then, one day he took his time. He didn't know why but this time he decided to take it easy. He was late getting to the airport that one day and missed the airplane. Later, the plane crashed and some of his colleagues were killed with all the other passengers onboard. Was he just lucky?

A few scientists believe that the only reason we go forward in time is because our brains are hardwired for "forward only". What if, sometimes, memory possession works both ways? What if information can travel from the future or a possible future in the form of magnetic resonance that can register in the minds of certain individuals? But, what if certain individuals create their own futures?

Remember in the previous chapter when we discussed how, according to the Heisenberg Uncertainty Principle, we influence reality through observation? What if some people can pick and choose, on a subconscious level, certain outcomes? What if they could influence probability? They didn't predict the outcome of a dice roll --- they made it happen! There exists a great deal of evidence (hundreds of Parapsychological experiments) to suggest that human beings can influence probability. It is possible that a human can consciously force a random state of reality into a state that favors a specific desire and/or chosen outcome.

Finally, we come to hyperspace. No, we're not jumping in the *Millennium Falcon* for a trip to the Death Star. We're going to discuss the possibility of higher dimensions again. Perhaps some people are more open to higher dimensions than others. These persons would have a more open mind than most people and wouldn't be quite so hardwired for three or four-dimensional thought. Time itself is thought to be the fourth dimension. Can some people see beyond three dimensions? Can they "remember" the future like we remember the past?

Perhaps, perhaps, perhaps. More research is definitely needed.

Poltergeists, the Real-Life "Entity" & a Ghost Named "Phillip"

Poltergeist Agent (PA): Phenomena usually surrounding a young child, which is usually a girl; the P.A. (the child) is almost always around when the poltergeist activity occurs; this usually involves objects being thrown around when there is no one around, unexplainable tapping and scratching noises and objects disappearing and reappearing hours, days or weeks later; in worst-case scenarios there can be injuries to human beings from thrown objects and scratches appearing on the flesh of the P.A.; fires are also known to occur in the worst cases - sometimes with catastrophic results.

Many parapsychologists today do not use the term *poltergeist* or *poltergeist agent*. They prefer *recurrent spontaneous psychokinesis* or RSPK. Why can't they just keep it simple! A poltergeist phenomenon is not ghost related at all. Unlike cases of hauntings (which can last for decades if not centuries) poltergeist phenomena doesn't last for very long. As of 1991, in half of all the hundreds of cases recorded, half of them lasted less than two months, with most of those lasting only a few weeks. In most of these cases, the activity surrounds an adolescent who seems to be under psychological stress.

In 1967 Germany, an 18-year-old secretary named Annemarie Schneider seemed to be the focus of a major poltergeist outbreak at the offices of the lawyer she worked for. The local electrical company was at a loss to explain major electrical disturbances throughout the building. Loud bangs and power outages wreaked havoc around the office. Ceiling lamps would sway back and forth, sometimes violently. Light bulbs exploded and electrical fuses blew for no apparent reason. Later, when poltergeist investigator Professor Hans Bender of the University of Freiburg visited the phenomena increased! Filing cabinets weighing more than 400 lbs moved from the wall and drawers opened by themselves. Only when Annemarie started at another job did the disturbances cease.

More recently, in 1984, there was a case of a poltergeist agent in Columbus, Ohio. John and Joan Resch were two remarkable people. By 1983, they had helped over 250 disturbed and homeless foster children! On any given day the house would have in it John and Joan Resch, their son Craig, their adopted daughter Tina (pictured) and maybe four or more foster kids.

The strange things that started happening in the Resch household began with all the lights in the household turning themselves off. All of them, all at once! An electrician was called in and he couldn't find anything wrong at all. It would get weirder.

Objects like clocks, candlesticks and pictures would leave their spots and fly through the air. Knives would fling themselves from their drawers and wine glasses would shatter. The shower would start running on its own and eggs would pop out of their carton and shoot up at the ceiling. Witnesses saw objects from other rooms fly into a room Tina was sitting in and smack into her. It quickly became obvious that Tina was the "focus" of this particular poltergeist phenomenon.

After a botched exorcism didn't work the Resch's were at their wits end. The house was a disaster zone from all the activity. Not just poltergeist activity either! By this time the place was full of reporters, policemen and firemen. One of these reporters would take a photo that would bring this story into national attention.

(photo Associated Press / Columbus Dispatch)

The picture appeared to show a phone fly on its own across Tina's lap. All the media attention peaked the interest of parapsychologist William Roll. Roll would become absolutely certain that this was a case of recurrent spontaneous psychokinesis or RSPK.

Later, however, Tina would be caught by a video camera that was left on by accident tugging a lamp cord to make the lamp appear to fly at her. Despite dozens of eyewitness accounts by many people who had nothing to gain by lying, skeptics would use the video evidence as a "smoking gun" to prove the whole thing was a hoax. Tina said she only started faking things to get the reporters out of the house. However, the damage was done.

The stress that seemed to have created the poltergeist focus in the first place never seemed to leave Tina's frail psyche even though the activity did. In 1994, at the age of 23, she was sentenced to life imprisonment for murdering her three-year-old daughter.

Stress and emotional "issues" seem deeply tied in with cases of poltergeist activity. Many poltergeist agents will notice a decline or complete stop in activity after receiving counseling. In some of the less common cases, the P.A. is actually able to manifest a consciously separate entity. Perhaps this entity is an incarnation of the P.A.'s own subconscious. Like the "id monster" from the movie *Forbidden Planet*, this manifestation is rarely benevolent. Some researchers, including myself, believe this is what may have happened in the famous real-life "Entity case". In this case, which took place in 1974, a poor, downtrodden woman named Doris Bither and her children experienced horrendous events at the hands of what appear to be Asian-looking phantoms. The events included violent rapes! This well documented case involved several paranormal investigators from UCLA who witnessed strange three-dimensional lights that would move through the room like the inside of a giant lava lamp. On another occasion, an apparition appeared at which point two investigators passed out. Could Doris and/or her children cause all this? Could the entities witnessed in fact be subconscious manifestations of Doris' own fears of rape and xenophobia?

You have to wonder how far can you take the concept of artificially created ghosts or "entities", subconscious or otherwise? Well, in 1972 members of the Toronto Society for Psychical Research and parapsychologists A.R.G. Owen and Iris M. Owen set out to create their own ghost! It would seem they accomplished this task without any of the members having any obvious paranormal sensitivity or psychic ability.

To begin this imaginative new experiment, they needed to create a history for their ghostly "Frankenstein's Monster." They named him "Philip", that is "Philip Aylesford". Philip had an elaborate history too:

- Born Philip Aylesford in 1624
- Joined the military at 15.
- Fought in the English Civil War between 1639 and 1640.
- Was knighted in 1640.
- Philip became friends with Prince Charles I.
- He then worked as a secret agent for Charles II.
- He knew Oliver Cromwell, the infamous English politician and soldier.

Phillip was also married but had an affair with a gypsy. When his wife found out about the affair, she accused the gypsy of witchcraft and had her burned at the stake. Philip could have intervened, but didn't. He killed himself out of guilt in 1654 at the age of 30. What a life, huh?

The society began having "séances" and tried to manifest an apparition through vivid concentration. Although some of the members claimed to feel a presence, nothing happened for months. They began table-tipping experiments based on research done by British psychologist Kenneth J. Batcheldor. Batcheldor believed that table-tipping was a form of telekinesis manifested from the belief of those present in séances and was not in fact "ghosts".

After three or four tries, they began to feel vibrations on the table. After awhile, the vibrations became taps and knocks and the table moved beneath their hands. A member of the team asked out loud if Philip had done the knocking and there was a loud rap that answered. Using one tap for "yes" and two taps for "no", the team was able to converse with their creation. It is interesting to note that the "spirit" could not answer questions outside of the history that was created for him.

The "haunting" escalated when Philip began greeting latecomers to the séances by moving the table toward them and sometime he'd even trap a team member in the corner with the table. He even tapped to the beat of music from time to time.

Communication with Philip continued for several years. Attempts were made to record Philip using EVP and they were somewhat successful. They thought they heard a lot of whispering with some clear responses. Interest in Philip finally waned in 1977 when no further progress was made in understanding the mechanics of the phenomena.

So, what is Psi? What is PK? Is it previously unknown form of energy or are the persons involved in these events manipulating reality and/or existing energy fields? There are more questions than answers right now and it might be a long time before we see any real answers. Much more research and study is need by newer and fresher investigators.

Psi Test

I created a test not too long ago based on testing done by parapsychologists. It is an HTML based test on the Baltimore Society for Paranormal Research website and can be found at **http://bsprnet.com/bspr/psi_test/.** On the site is a random number generator composed of a single integer. According to the laws of averages, when you refresh your browser you have a 50/50 chance of getting a 1 or a 0. Theoretically, if you refreshed your browser 100 times you should get approximately 50 zeros and 50 ones. Give or take only a few. Go further and 1000 refreshes should get you 500 zeros and 500 ones with a slightly larger margin of error.

It is an experiment in micro-PK to see if you can affect the outcome of the integer. Take a piece of paper, preferably a large one, put it to the side. You will need to focus on 1 or 0. Focus as hard as you can. Then start refreshing your browser. Every time you refresh the browser, score your paper. If you score your paper 10 times it should look like this:

So, one score for every refresh. Got it? Above each group of scores write the number of times your chosen number came up. For example: If your chosen number was 0 and 0 came up five times out of ten as odds are they will, it may look like this:

Suffice to say, if you are powerfully psychic, then you should beat the 50/50 odds with a high margin. For example: If you chose 0 and 0 came up 60% of the time, you may be powerfully psychic or at least unusually lucky. Or you can simply flip a coin a bunch of times.

Do You See Dead People?

So, you have a team of ghost hunters or you are on a team of ghost hunters.....

If you do not already have someone who claims to be a sensitive on your team, someone will come along. Trust me. It is as Agent Smith told Neo "an inevitability". But how do you tell a real sensitive from a fraud or someone who exaggerates his or her talents? Well, it depends on whether you want to be taken seriously or not.

I have come across three disturbing situations when it comes to team sensitives:

1. The team has on it a sensitive that is a fraud or exaggerates his/her abilities and doesn't care to do anything about it.

2. The team has on it a sensitive that is a fraud or exaggerates his/her abilities and exploits their flamboyant personality for personal gain (i.e. media coverage, etc.).

3. The team has on it a sensitive that is a fraud or exaggerates his/her abilities and the team relies completely on this person since they do not know any better.

But how do you know any better? How do you decide if the person who says they are a sensitive is a sensitive? Well, it's not easy, but I'll give you some hints.

1. Are they very flamboyant? Look for the clichés! Do they wander around saying they feel the presence of famous historical figures or celebrities. "I smell peanut butter and bananas! The King is here!" Do they hyperventilate when a powerful "energy/entity" is present? You have to determine if they are really sick from their over sensitivity or are they "I want to go home from school early to play video games" sick (i.e. faking it).

2. Can they determine real history from a location without previous knowledge? Take them to a place where they don't or couldn't have known the area's history, but you do. See if they can figure out details about names and events by themselves.

3. Are they uncreative in their "made-up" histories? I have been on several investigations with other teams that have, possibly, a bad sensitive. With one team there seemed to be an abundance of "Sarahs" around. "I feel the presence of someone named Sarah," she said at one Civil War era location. "Someone is calling to me... Her name is Sarah," she said at a colonial-era location. Also, with some there seems to be an abundance of slave ghosts in Civil War era locations. Even in places that history says there were no slaves!

So, how do you spot a real sensitive?

1. They are not flamboyant. Most sensitives are nervous about talking about their "gift". You may have to quiz someone who starts acting a little strangely in haunted locations. Sometimes they will not volunteer information unless asked.

2. They can reveal details about a location's history in advance of actually knowing. This is almost always a sure sign. If you take someone into an obscure location (i.e. somewhere not mentioned often on the History Channel) how can they know its historical information in advance?

3. They have an annoying tendency to wander off by themselves. Those that I believe are truly sensitive seem to do this all the time. I think it may be because other people sometimes distract and that they don't want people staring at them. They have to be reminded of safety though.

At the Maryland Paranormal Investigators Coalition (MD-PIC) we do use sensitives on investigations of ghosts and hauntings. However, we keep their identities private. We do not go around saying, "This is [CENSORED], our team psychic." There are several reasons for this anonymity:

1. The media has a tendency to ridicule people who claim to be "psychic". No matter how much you try to claim to the press that your group uses the latest in scientific theories to examine the phenomena of ghosts, you will surprised how much focus the will made on your group's sensitive. Then you will be surprised about how much sarcasm makes its way into the final report.

2. Ego. There is a risk that the person in question may become to big for his/her britches. Anonymity will help prevent a need to exaggerate to please an audience.

3. Discomfort from residential owners or property managers. You are being invited into the homes and property of people who may be scared already. They are probably uncomfortable having a team of ghost hunters in their house and are possibly hoping you will find a "natural" "non-paranormal" explanation for what's going on. They may be uncomfortable with the idea of their being a psychic on the team. It is best to not even ask.

There seems to be an increase in the amount of people claiming to be sensitives in the field of ghost research these days. Are we headed into a resurgence of the Spiritualist movement? Probably not.

It is possible that there are many people out there who have had these "feelings" but have not been aware of what they are until they caught those "ghost shows" on cable. Also, I have little doubt there are persons out there with low self-esteem that are taking advantage of naïve new groups of ghost investigators. Just use caution.

7. THE FUTURE OF GHOST HUNTING

"If you want to know your future, look at what you are doing in this moment."
– Tibetan Proverb

"Even the smallest person can change the course of the future.'"
– Galadrial to Frodo the Hobbit in the "Lord of the Rings"

What does the future of ghost hunting hold for us? A lot, I hope! It is now the 21st century and there is a new generation of ghost hunters out there, pioneering new techniques and technologies that have never been tried before!

Biofeedback

A new technique being used by the Maryland Paranormal Investigators Coalition is utilizing biological feedback from the investigators themselves!

We have hooked up both sensitive and non-sensitive investigators to a heart-rate/blood pressure monitor and a body voltage sensor attached to a standard Multimeter. The body voltage meter checks the electrical resistance of your body against any electrical current in the air. An external electric field will induce an electric field within our bodies. In this sense, our bodies act as antennas picking up fields from all kinds of sources. Delicate biological cellular processes (like brain function and heart muscle contraction) operate on the scale of microvolts. Simply touch this sensor with a finger and know instantly what effect external fields are having inside your body.

I have been talking about how environments must be altered when affected by an outside stimulus such as ghosts. Well, what about the effects of ghosts on the human beings? We have all heard of people being affected emotionally by certain kids of hauntings (i.e. feelings of dread, sadness, even extreme happiness, etc.), but how does a haunting affect someone physiologically? This is the purpose of this experiment.

In the future I imagine using an EKG for this type of an experiment.

An EKG (or Electrocardiogram) is a diagnostic test that analyzes the electrical activity of the heart. A brainwave monitor would also be great for this. These sorts of apparatus have been used in psi-testing for years. In the 21st century, I can see them being used for ghost hunting as well.

Robotics

Ta-da! Presenting the *Ghost Tech Robo-Cam*! I built it from all-terrain R/C truck parts. It has four-wheel drive, stainless steel spring-loaded shocks, all-terrain puncture proof tires, sensor array (compass, clock and temperature gauge), a 2.4-gigahertz wireless infrared camera and mounts for another camera or other peripherals. Its low profile allows going into places people couldn't otherwise go into. I used R/C truck parts instead of R/C car parts because car parts are less agile and go too fast. What good is a robotic surveillance device that drives around at scale 120 mph? You'll miss everything!

The reason I designed and built this little guy (we consider "him" a member of the team and refer to him as a "he") was to go into places that would be much too dangerous for a person to go into. Now, I don't mean the dark closet where Max Shrek's *Nosferatu* is hiding and waiting to attack an innocent ghost hunter..... I mean places with weak floorboards, small crawlspaces and unsafe mines. We have also built a *Blimp-Cam* to go on investigations where locations may be even too rough or inaccessi-

ble for the Robo-Cam. I got the idea for the Blimp-Cam from a location in Maryland's Ellicott City. The Patapsco Female Institute is supposed to be haunted by a little girl who died at the school. She is said to stare out the second story window with dark, sad eyes. However, as you can see from this picture, there is no second floor! A fire gutted the institute years ago. What better way to investigate a non-existent second floor than with a flying remote controlled video camera? We have only used it on the *USS Constellation* as of yet.

A colleague of mine in Pennsylvania named Craig Teleshe has built his own robotic ghost hunter. Craig owns **www.ghost-tech.com** and has built a very impressive robotic monitoring system himself! Ghunter (Ghost + Hunter): the robotic paranormal investigator!

From Craig's website:

"Ghunter started his life as a Hero Jr. robot, designed by Heathkit in the early 80s as a robotic companion. Unfortunately the processor of this Hero Jr. was fried when I received him, so all I was left with was a base with wheels and a drive system and a power supply board. He sat in my basement for a while till I came up with this grand idea! What if I could use the base and mount a video camera on top of it to be used ghost investigations.

"After a few different design ideas, a dozen trips to Radio Shack and a months work, Ghunter was up and running. Ghunter has the following functions:

- Digital Radio control at 433 Mhz
- 8mm Camcorder modified to see in near darkness (infrared).
- Digital camera, which can be activated via radio control.
- Infrared motion detector, which can activate the digital camera.
- A sixteen LED infrared emitter. (Creates a very nice bright picture)
- Mini Pinhole camera for remote viewing of robot functions on receiver.
- 2.4 GHz video transmitter hooked to the Pinhole camera.

"The transmitter controls the drive system to move the robot, a button to activate the digital camera remotely, activates the infrared system, which will take pictures when motion is detected (don't want to be driving the robot around when this is active of course) and activates the infrared LEDs on front of the robot If lighting conditions are too low.

"Ghunter's power system is 2 large 13-amp 6-volt batteries wired in series to produce 12 volts. These batteries will run all of the devices and the robot for about 6 hours which it plenty of time to conduct an investigation. I have not officially taken Ghunter out on and investigation yet, but his time is coming."

Now Ghunter is a little too bulky for dangerous locations with weak floorboards and small crawl spaces, but it does serve another purpose: remote observation of locations without a human presence.

Have you ever heard of a place that where more activity happens when the family goes out then when they were home? How about the family that didn't even know there was a ghost in their home until someone took a picture of the front of the house and saw a ghostly face in the window when the pictures were developed? It happens. The Ghost Tech Ghost-Cam, Blimp-Cam and Ghunter are the first in what is no doubt part of the future of robotic ghost hunting!

Ghost Tech

A few years ago, Stan Suho developed the *Geophysically Equipped Instrument of Scientific Testing* --- otherwise known as G.E.I.S.T. What Suho had done was design a computer-based monitoring system capable of monitoring, recording and testing the environment without the bothersome presence of human beings. Using a "polling device", Suho was able to attach multiple instruments (EMF meters, Geiger Counters, Thermometers, etc.) to a single laptop. Recently Justin Faulk of **www.ghostgadgets.com** has gone one step further.

Justin developed ARCADIA or the Analog Reading Computer Aided Digital Input Analyzer. From Justin's website:

"There have been several other scientific based groups that have interfaced computer logging systems to natural field meters before, but ARCADIA takes it a step further. All previous systems of its kind have only logged continuous streams of data, leaving hours of digital or analog data to sort through. Personally, I hate data review, so I have someone else do it for me --- the computer, in real time. Data from each channel is sent through a device-specific algorithm, developed from hundreds of hours of control runs. With this algorithm, Arcadia can actively distinguish what should naturally occur in a given field (static magnetic fields, temperature, humidity, etc.), and therefore can ignore the data in a stable environment. When an anomaly becomes apparent to the system, Arcadia will log the data from the anomaly digitally, which can be further analyzed later." Mr. Faulk adds, "Now, Arcadia has been modified to log everything for specific time blocks, do various types of DSP on the data sets, and calculate statistical data for each block (standard deviation, mean, range, etc.). That way, a true mathematical analysis canbe implemented, including probability values, etc., for submission to peer reviewed journals."

Cataloging Data

The better groups of ghost hunters and investigators of the strange and unusual are pioneering new techniques and technologies to find the answer to the ultimate question. No, it's not 42.

Are ghost real?

Keeping your information to yourself isn't going to help anyone. Not even you. You need to share. Also, you will need to keep very good notes and absolute control over your investigation. As I mentioned before, the Maryland Paranormal Investigators Coalition has developed some very good forms for cataloging data on hauntings. I strongly suggest that you download those forms or create your own. Forms and ruled notebooks will keep your notes nice and tidy. When I first started, I used to have wads of paper in my pockets with all my notes on them. Now, I bring a tote bag with clipboards and extra pens.

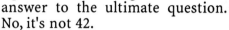

Some researchers into the paranormal are researchers in other fields as well. Recently I have been discussing techniques with a teacher of archeology and the techniques they use to document areas in digs and historical investigations. I hope that ghost investigating will become more commonplace and more acceptable. It would be great if more members of the scientific community would become interested in ghost hunting.

8. THEORIES FROM THE PROS

An idea, like a ghost, must be spoken to a little before it will explain itself.
- Charles Dickens (famous British author)

A ghost is someone who hasn't made it - in other words, who died, and they don't know they're dead. So they keep walking around and thinking that you're inhabiting their... let's say, their domain. So they're aggravated with you.
- Sylvia Brown (self-proclaimed psychic and medium)

I believe a ghost is the consciousness or essence of someone who once lived. This (soul) survives the physical body and retains its intelligence and emotions, and can manifest through sight, sound, touch, scent, and presence.
- Rick Fisher (Founder of the Paranormal Society of Pennsylvania)

With this book, I have tried to submit to the public theories on the nature of ghosts and hauntings. My hope is that someone in the scientific community will read these theories and be inspired to do some real research into the reality of ghosts. Suffice to say, realistically, I will probably be experiencing the reality of ghosts first-hand before that ever happens

I have submitted to the readers of this book a few theories, a lot of science and some history too. However, these are not the be all and end all of theories that exist. Opinions are like well, you know.... I mean everyone has their own opinion on what exactly ghosts may or may not be. For example, I have pooled the ghost hunting community in search for theories of other well-seasoned investigators and paranormal specialists. What do some of the most well known ghost hunters, my friends and colleagues, in the country think ghosts may be?

Charles J. Adams III

Charles J. Adams III was born in Reading, Pennsylvania, in 1947 and resides there today. In addition to his books, Adams also writes regular features on travel and local legends in the *Reading Eagle* newspaper and

has written travel stories for several other magazines and publications.

Adams has been a speaker at the International Ghost Hunters Alliance conventions in Gettysburg, Pa., and has been interviewed on ghostly topics in England, Ireland, South Africa, and on several American radio and television stations.

He has also appeared on The History Channel's "Haunted America: New York" and "Haunted America: Philadelphia" programs and has served as consultant and on-air "expert" for programs on hauntings and ghosts on The Learning Channel, MTV, and The Travel Channel. He is presently involved in the production of a segment on haunted Broadway theaters for the A&E network.

Adams has also organized and escorted tours of haunted places in the United States, England, and Scotland.

He has produced, written, and conducted "ghost tours" in Lancaster County, Reading, and Philadelphia, Pa.; Cape May, N.J., and Greenwich Village, New York City. His stories have been selected for inclusion in such books as "Classic American Ghost Stories" (August House Publishing) and "HexCraft" (Llewellyn Publications). His book, "Bucks County Ghost Stories" was used as a prop in the 2002 movie, "Signs," which stars Mel Gibson.

What does Charles say?

We humans are made of flesh and blood...and electrical energy.

It is that energy that sparks and stimulates our nervous system, our brain waves, our intellect, and our imagination.

Upon death, the flesh rots, the blood dries, but the energy, I believe, is expelled from the corporeal case it inhabited and is dispersed into the environment. Some of it is deposited on some sort of medium (rust? iron ore?) that retains the energy-including bits and pieces of thoughts, emotions, and shards of discursive and communicative faculties.

This "recording" can then be "played back" by a receptive individual by intent or by accident. A "ghost" truly takes shape when other baseline factors such as historical documentation are incorporated with this raw, stored energy.

Rosemary Ellen Guiley

Rosemary Ellen Guiley works full-time as a paranormal researcher, investigator and author. She was born in Florida and grew up in Seattle

and Anchorage. She earned a BA in Communications from the University of Washington and went to work as a news journalist. After moving to New York State, she was able to realize my dream of becoming a full-time author. Her specialization: the paranormal, which has fascinated her all of her life.

Rosemary's work in the paranormal has led her into intense study, research and investigation of a wide range of topics, which she has featured in more than 30 books and encyclopedias, hundreds of articles and numerous presentations. Along the way she has had many experiences that have illuminated some of the mysteries of the multiverse -- the multi-dimensional universe of which we are a part.

Rosemary has written for FATE magazine since 1991 and is currently consulting editor. In 2000, she formed Visionary Living, Inc. as a media company for her work. In 2001, she obtained a PhD from the International Institute for Integral Human Sciences in Montreal.

Rosemary makes her home in Maryland, and travels a great deal to do research and make public appearances. She has also added acting to my activities, appearing in films with paranormal themes.

What does Rosemary say?

I believe there are various explanations for ghosts, and that no one theory explains them all. In addition to the usual theories - trapped spirits or recordings in etheric space - here is one seldom discussed:

What if ghosts - or some ghosts - are created not by the dead, but by the living?

Consider, for example, a haunting involving a tragedy, such as a violent death by accident or murder. In this scenario, the emotions of living persons have enough force to construct a ghost of the victim. Emotional fuel comes from trauma of those personally involved, as well as from intense and morbid interest from the curious.

Such a ghost is a type of thought-form. The thought-form takes hold in the astral plane, which can be accessed psychically by the living, sometimes through deliberate clairvoyance and sometimes spontaneously through natural, inborn psi. The thought-form ghost gains strength from the continual emotions and interest of the living and takes on a life of its own. Thought-forms with less power become like recordings.

Many ghosts seem to run out of energy after a few months or years, while others last for centuries. The ability of a thought-form to survive depends on variable factors, none of which are predictable:
- The ongoing, collective thoughts and feelings of the living who tune

in by visiting a haunted place, and to a lesser extent, reading about it;
- Geophysical properties of the site that may contribute to paranormal phenomena;
- Unknown factors in the astral plane.
I do not think that we, the living, deliberately create ghosts. Rather, they may spring forth from us unconsciously, perhaps as a way of keeping memories of the past alive.

Loyd Auerbach

Loyd Auerbach, M.S., is the Director of the Office of Paranormal Investigations, an adjunct Professor at JFK University and just finished his fourth (and final) year as President of the international organization, the Psychic Entertainers Association. He is a past President (and currently Vice President) of the California Society for Psychical Study and on the advisory board of the Rhine Research Center of Durham, NC.

Auerbach holds a degree in Cultural Anthropology from Northwestern University and a graduate degree in Parapsychology from JFK University.

He is creator and principal instructor of the new Parapsychological Studies Certification Program at HCH Institute in Lafayette, CA, and a new website Invisible Signals, an audio newsletter of the paranormal (www.invisiblesignals.com)

He is the author of several books and audio CDs. His most recent book is *A Paranormal Casebook: Ghost Hunting in the New Millennium* from Atriad Press, compiling many of his most interesting case investigations. In 2004, he released *Ghost Hunting: How to Investigate the Paranormal, and Hauntings* and *Poltergeists: The Ghost Hunter's Guide.* Both are from Ronin Publishing, 2004.

His first book, *ESP, Hauntings and Poltergeists* was named the "Sacred Text" on Ghosts by NEWSWEEK In 1996.

He was a columnist and consulting editor for FATE magazine from 1991 through 2004. He is a professional speaker on the college circuit, with his presentation True Tales of Ghosts and Hauntings. In addition, he lectures on a variety of other paranormally related topics.

He is a professional mentalist and psychic entertainer, performing as Professor Paranormal for all sorts of audiences, from small private parties to large corporate, college and public events.

Loyd Auerbach has appeared on hundreds of radio shows, and dozens of local and national TV shows, including *Larry King Live, Unsolved*

Mysteries, The Today Show, OPRAH, Sightings, Popular Mechanics for Kids, Coast to Coast with Art Bell and Late Night with David Letterman.. He is constantly haunting occasional new shows and many re-runs on the Discovery Channel, the Travel Channel, Tech-TV, the Travel Channel, A&E, the History Channel and The Learning Channel. He is featured in and was Series Consultant for the Travel Channel mini-series *"America's Most Haunted Places."* He is co-producer for and appears on camera in the video documentary *The Haunting of the USS Hornet.*

Loyd Auerbach has been conducting his investigations and research in the world of psychic phenomena and the paranormal for over 25 years.
- The Office of Paranormal Investigations, PO Box 875, Orinda, CA 94563-0875
- 415-249-9275.
- Email for Loyd Auerbach: esper@california.com
- Visit the Paranormal Network website at www.mindreader.com

What does Loyd say?

Most of us who approach ghosts from a Parapsychological perspective find a difference between the interactive, apparently conscious apparitions and the more repetitive phenomena that seem to be place specific.

An apparition, or discarnate entity, is our personality (or spirit, soul, consciousness, mind or whatever you want to call it) surviving the death of the body, and capable of interaction with the living (and presumably other apparitions). Apparitions are essentially pure consciousness. They interact with others (living and deceased) through some form of telepathic process (mind to mind) and with the environment through other psychic processes (perceptual and psychokinetic).

The more common (significantly so) kind of ghost experience is a result of hauntings or place memory. The environment somehow captures information as time progresses. Human beings are capable of perceiving some of this stored information, with our perceptions playing back bits and pieces from the past (including the recent past -- not just old history). A haunting is essentially a recording of some past person(s) or event(s). Magnetic fields are linked more strongly to hauntings than to apparitions.

Both apparitions and hauntings may be experienced through what appears to be our normal senses, but what actually is how our perceptual processes convert the data we receive from the place or the entity. One may appear much like the other. What separates an apparition from a haunting ghost is that idea of interaction. If a haunting is like a replay of videotape, an apparition is a video conference call. While speaking to the videotape brings no response, the conference call allows for two-way communication.

And then there are poltergeists, a class all on their own...

Robbin Van Pelt

Robbin has been involved with the paranormal since she 1984.

A series of strange coincidences occurred after her grandmother passed that made her go hhmm? She began reading everything she could get her hands on to learn more about the subject.

It wasn't until she met Martha Neidert, the mother of her good friend Katie, that things really took off for what would be a newfound career.

Martha had just published her 1st book on angels. Robbin spent the next 3 years learning about the other side of life (the afterlife) through Martha. When Martha passed on from cancer a few years ago Robbin promised to continue on and find the answers others seek to understand about spirits.

Robbin is a professional photographer with a background in electronics, digital imaging and video work. She now uses these skills to help MD-PIC, BSPR, BCPR/GDPI and the American Battlefield Ghost Hunters Society.

Robbin was just published in her first book written by Lynda Lee Macken called *Haunted Baltimore*. Robbin is also mentioned in Ed Okonowicz's book *Baltimore Ghosts*. She was also in the October 2004 issue of *Baltimore Magazine* along with Vince Wilson and Mary DuVall and is credited in Vince Wilson's *Ghost Tech*, which was published in 2005.

What does Robbin Say?

What are ghosts? That is the big question. If we knew what ghosts really were then there wouldn't be such a quest to find them. No one really knows, we can only speculate.

I myself seem to learn towards the theory that ghosts are spirits of those who have left this world and the soul, which is energy, lives on. We know energy cannot be destroyed, so at death is our souls energy transformed? We know we can measure this energy with instruments such as an EMF meter and Tri-field meters.

The emotions and intelligence that make up who we were in life seems to survive after death. Some have elected to remain others have been forced to. They maybe stuck here for reasons such as tragic sudden death, fear of moving on, guilt or unfinished business. Maybe they are here visiting loved ones or to warn them or pass along a message.

From the spirits I have encountered all of them are relatively harmless.

In extreme cases they may cause dangerous situations but this is not normal it is actually rare.

Think about the fact that they see you, you don't see them so they will try to get your attention however they can. They turn lights, TVs, and radios on and off, they move things. They make noise, sounds, footsteps, and you may even hear voices. You may smell perfume, cigars, and smoke. You may feel cold or cold spots. You may have the sensation of being touched or pushed. The spirit could just be a prankster. Maybe you are changing their homes and they want you to stop it. Perhaps they just want you to leave their home. Any of these events can make it scary or terrifying for people.

George Hanson

George P. Hansen was professionally employed in parapsychology laboratories for eight years-three at the Rhine Research Center in Durham, North Carolina, and five at Psychophysical Research Laboratories in Princeton, New Jersey.

His experiments included remote viewing, card guessing, ganzfeld, electronic random number generators, séance phenomena, and ghosts. He has been active in a number of psychic, UFO, and New Age organizations, and he helped found a skeptics group.

His papers in scientific journals cover mathematical statistics, fraud and deception, the skeptics' movement, conjurors in parapsychology, and exposés of hoaxes. He is a member of the International Brotherhood of Magicians.

What does George say?

Laboratory-based parapsychology research has shown that psychic phenomena are shaped by observers' expectations, personality characteristics, and beliefs ? all of which are heavily influenced by culture. These same factors also seem to affect ghostly manifestations, so we need to recognize our culture's impact on the manifestations. We should ponder not just the putative phenomena themselves, but also the conditions surrounding them ? including the peculiarities faced by ghost researchers. For instance:

- For thousands of years ghosts have been reported, discussed, and denied. Today the debates over their existence are as heated as ever. The disputes show no sign of being resolved.
- Movies such as *The Sixth Sense, Ghost,* and *Ghostbusters* have been

immensely popular. Each has taken in hundreds of millions of dollars in box office receipts. In contrast, for the past quarter century the average support for serious ghost research published in refereed, scientific, English-language journals is probably less than $10,000 annually.

- No scientific institutions (with offices, buildings, paid staff) are devoted to investigating the reality of ghosts. There are virtually no university courses on ghost research, and there is no credible academic textbook on the topic.

- Those who try to investigate the phenomena are likely to be housewives, police officers, or college students working on their own nickel, with no support from any institution.

- Active ghost research groups rarely last for more than a few years. Such organizations frequently fractionate and dissolve, leaving behind feelings of bitterness and disappointment.

- Conferences devoted to ghosts often include presentations on UFOs, Bigfoot, aliens, and channelers. The boundaries between these topics are blurred.

- Many people will speak of their ghost experiences, but often only in hushed tones, and maybe only to close friends. They perceive a stigma associated with the phenomena.

The above facts are well known to ghost researchers, but they are rarely, if ever, incorporated into theories of ghosts. Yet any comprehensive theory must explain these conditions. But how are we to make sense of them?

Anthropologists' concept of liminality may help because it addresses phenomena that are ambiguous and paradoxical. The word liminal comes from limen, meaning threshold, and liminality refers to the condition of being betwixt and between. It was derived from analyses of rites of passage. In fact, anthropologists report that in earlier cultures, novices in ritual initiations were frequently likened to ghosts, gods, and ancestors.

Liminality theory is founded on understandings of earlier cultures, which recognized, and respected, the reality of ghosts. The concept is not well known, and it's likely to be foreign to nearly all persons involved with parapsychology or ghost research. Nevertheless, this anthropological theory has innumerable implications for paranormal fields.

Liminal phenomena are typically transient, ephemeral, and have an affinity for chaos, transition, and instability. They are also usually viewed as slightly disreputable. Ghosts themselves are transient; their manifestations are unpredictable. They are neither solid nor stable. The question of their reality is perennially in dispute. Marginality is a type of liminality, and ghost research is viewed as exceedingly marginal, even laughable, by the scientific establishment.

Ghosts are ambiguous; they are a betwixt and between phenomenon.

For instance, are they alive? Or are they dead? Are they fact? Or are they fiction? Are they natural? Or supernatural? Hallucinations? Or real? Ghosts blur these distinctions. They are encompassed by all these categories but are firmly in none. They lie in between these assorted classifications.

Various liminal (and psychic) phenomena tend to blur together. This is true of ghosts. Some suggest that ghosts are telepathic hallucinations. Others ask whether spirits exist as independent entities, or if they are products of human psychic abilities (e.g., unconscious clairvoyant or psychokinetic abilities of observers). Professional parapsychologists are still undecided whether there is any real difference between ESP and psychokinesis. These issues of "blurred categories" have been argued for more than a century in psychical research.

Anti-structure is a synonym of liminality in anthropological theory. The word reflects the transitory, unstable nature of ghost research groups. Direct attempts to engage the phenomena have side effects; they often lead to (or reflect) instability in the lives of people and groups in the vicinity.

Space is severely limited here, and the full scope of the theory cannot be presented briefly. The concept is abstract, and my presentation has risked giving a too-limited overview. Readers wishing more discussion might peruse my article "Ghosts and Liminality" and the Introduction to my book, *The Trickster and the Paranormal*. Both can be found on my website -- **www.tricksterbook.com**

Jaime Lee Henkin

A native of Baltimore, Jaime Henkin has had an unquenchable curiosity of the history and folklore of the area since early childhood. In childhood, a combination of personal experiences, Scooby-Doo, Daniel Cohen, and bad horror movies lead to a fascination with the paranormal. By the time she was in high school, Jaime was attending informal ghost hunts, lectures, and recording every episode of Sightings.

Jaime took her interests in history and the paranormal to the next level in 1998 and founded Baltimore County Paranormal Research (BCPR), the group formerly known as Greater Dundalk Paranormal Investigators.

In 1999 she joined the American Ghost Society and soon thereafter became an Area Representative for Baltimore. Jaime was invited to join the Maryland Paranormal

Investigators Coalition in 2002 and is the current Vice President.

Jaime has lectured on various paranormal topics and is currently working on a book specific to paranormal activity in and around Baltimore.

Outside of paranormal investigation, Jaime is a published poet who dabbles in short stories. She also has many other interests including travel (to haunted places of course), reading, antiques, and collecting just about everything.

Jaime lives in her hometown, Dundalk, Maryland, with her husband, Josh, a few cats and a Yorky named Candy who thinks she rules the world.

What does Jaime say?

When asked what I think ghosts are, I inwardly cringe out of sympathy for the questioner. I just can't answer that question simply because my mind instantly springs forth a dozen theories, such as the "conventional" idea that ghosts are the souls of the deceased to the more "controversial" concept that ghosts are an experience caused by certain environmental factors. I have a reason why each theory is plausible and a reason why each theory is inherently flawed. I always seem to be the Devils' Advocate, even with myself.

If I had to pick a favorite theory, it would be that ghosts are created by a release of energy (the "soul") from the human body after death and its subsequent attachment to a location or object. This energy attachment could potentially maintain many characteristics of the individual, interact with the environment, and cause certain emotional or physical reactions in those who enter the environment. Perhaps this could also explain why ghosts don't "appear" to everyone. Maybe some individuals are just more sensitive to this energy attachment, much like some people are more sensitive to vibrations, scents, light, or sound.

No matter what ghosts are, I just know that they are not "paranormal" or "supernatural" in nature because by their very existence they have to obey the laws of the universe. The First Law of Thermodynamics leaves wide open the possibility of ghosts by stating that energy cannot be created nor destroyed, but only change form. When we die does our personality/soul/life force change into what we refer to as a ghost? But then why doesn't everyone become a ghost? And I'll stop there before I write a book of my own.

Even though I would love to know what ghosts are, in a way I hope that we don't explain their existence in my lifetime. Putting a ghost under a microscope, so to speak, takes all the mystery out of it. However, I don't think this is a danger. Mainstream science is a long way from ready to accept the existence ghosts, no matter what they are.

Troy Taylor

Troy Taylor is the author of more than 40 books about ghosts and hauntings in America, including *Haunted Illinois, The Ghost Hunter's Guidebook* and many others. He is also the editor of Ghosts of the Prairie Magazine and the president of the "American Ghost Society", a network of ghost hunters, which boasts more than 600 active members in the United States and Canada. The group collects stories of ghost sightings and haunted houses and uses investigative techniques to track down evidence of the supernatural. In addition, he also hosts a National Conference each year in conjunction with the group, which usually attracts several hundred ghost-enthusiasts from around the country.

Along with writing about ghosts, Taylor is also a public speaker on the subject and has spoken to hundreds private and public groups on a variety of paranormal subjects. He has appeared in literally dozens of newspaper and magazine articles about ghosts and hauntings. He has also been fortunate enough to be interviewed hundreds of times for radio and television broadcasts about the supernatural. He has also appeared in a number of documentary films and one feature film about the supernatural.

Born and raised in Illinois, Taylor has long had an affinity for "things that go bump in the night", he started his first ghost tour company in 1994 and published his first book a year later. Taylor is also the founder, co-owner and manager of the Illinois Hauntings Tour Co., with ghost tours in Alton, Decatur, Chicago and Springfield and of the Bump in the Night Tour Co., which offers haunted overnight stays at some of the most haunted places in America.

He currently resides in Illinois in a decidedly non-haunted house.

What does Troy say?
What is a ghost? Why do places become haunted?

I wish that I could say.... but no one really knows. And to be honest, I refuse to try and say one way or another. I have always been about presenting the evidence and allowing the individual to judge for himself.

It's my personal belief that there are a variety of different kinds of ghosts and hauntings. I believe in the discarnate spirits who are the personalities of those who once lived and have stayed behind for one reason or another. I also believe (very strongly) in the presence of "residual hauntings", those electrical memories that appear to be spirits but are actually just recordings of events gone by. Those are some of my personal beliefs but that's all they are, "personal beliefs."

Why am I so hesitant to try and push my own theories on the reader, you might ask?

There are so many types of hauntings, from human spirits to animals ghosts to even ghost ships, that no one has ever been able to come up with a theory to explain them all. A single theory would have to cover an immense variety of phenomena and it just can't be done. Such a theory would have to explain why apparitions are seen in one location, but not in others. It would have to provide a solution for phantom footsteps, cold spots, strange smells and much more. Developing such a theory is no easy matter, especially as few researchers can really agree about what underlying force causes a haunting in the first place.

Many authorities on the subject do not believe that ghosts are literally the "spirits" of people who have died and who have remained behind at a location. While it is a popular belief, many parapsychologists refuse to take it seriously. This is not to say that they reject the possibility that some hauntings are caused by the activities of the dead though. They just don't believe that the ghosts themselves are the actual forms of the dead.

Here's why: they use as an example that many haunted houses show no evidence that a past tragedy or death has taken place in them. And they also add that no evidence exists in many locations to say that any past personality is present there. The house might be haunted, but they don't believe that it is by the spirit of a dead person.

To be honest, I can't say that I agree with this, but I ask the reader to simply judge for himself. I agree that many locations do not boast events that might spawn ghosts, but isn't it possible that the ghosts may have stayed behind for other reasons altogether?

I have always felt there are many reasons for hauntings, so the idea that a ghost (or type of haunting) could be a single, all encompassing thing is a nice idea, but an unrealistic one. Even the word "ghost" is misleading. We use it as a generic term to describe both "spirits" and "apparitions", paranormal manifestations that are actually very different things.

There seem to be several different kinds of paranormal events that have been linked to ghosts. Are they all the work of the spirits? Your own investigations will have to decide that for you. I have seen and have experienced some things that I certainly feel were paranormal. On two occasions I believe that I actually saw ghosts and have been in a number of places where I believe that ghosts were present, based on the sounds and sensations that I and others present experienced.

With that said, I never claim to have all of the answers when it comes to ghosts. I simply digest the facts, theories and evidence and then use that information in conjunction with my own ideas and research. I suggest that every reader does the same. Just remember to accept all theories as possible, but question each one of them before accepting them as the truth.

Ursula Bielski

Historian, author, and parapsychology enthusiast, Ursula Bielski has been writing and lecturing about Chicago's supernatural folklore and the paranormal for more than 16 years. A recognized authority on the Chicago region's ghost-lore and cemetery history, she is the author of four popular and critically acclaimed books on the subject.

Ursula's interests in ghost hunting began at a young age. She grew up in a haunted house on Chicago's north side and received an early education in Chicago history from her father, a Chicago police officer. Since that time she has been involved in numerous investigations of haunted sites in and around Chicago, including such notorious locales as Wrigley Field; the Country House Restaurant in Clarendon Hills, IL; Chicago's Red Lion Pub; Bachelor's Grove Cemetery; and the Oshkosh, WI, Opera House.

Aside from her writing, Ursula has been featured on several television documentaries, including productions by the A&E Network, The History Channel, The Learning Channel, The Travel Channel, and PBS. She also appears regularly on local Chicago television and radio, and lectures throughout the year at various libraries, historical and professional societies. In addition to her books, Ursula is the author of numerous scholarly articles exploring the links between history and the paranormal, including articles published in the International Journal of Parapsychology.

Ursula is a past editor of PA News, the quarterly newsletter of the Parapsychological Association, a past president and board member of the Pi Gamma Chapter of Phi Alpha Theta, the national history honor society, and has membership in the Society of Midland Authors.

A graduate of St. Benedict High School in Chicago, Ursula holds a B.A. degree in history from Benedictine University and an M.A. in American cultural and intellectual history from Northeastern Illinois University. Her academic explorations include the spiritualist movement of the 19th century and its transformation into psychical research and parapsychology; and the relationship between belief, experience, science, and religion.

Ursula currently resides in Chicago.

What does Ursula say?

Anyone who's done investigations with me can tell you that I'm one of the sissiest ghost hunters you'll ever work with. You'll always find me asking another investigator to "Come with me to check out the upstairs" or to "hold this flashlight for me." Part of this trepidation stems, I'm sure, from my Catholic upbringing and its attendant world of demons. A bigger part comes from the fact that, after years and years of investigating the paranormal, I still have no idea where these phenomena come from. With that unknown, of course, comes terror.

Like most ghost hunters, I've come to believe that there are a wide variety of phenomena that we term "paranormal" and that there are nearly as many explanations for these phenomena as there are those who experience them. After scores of investigations--and my own experiences at home and elsewhere--and after observing the mechanics of supernatural experience working in our "Chicago Hauntings" tour guests, I have come to realize, however, that we, the living, have an awful lot to do with what we experience ... or do we?

In college, a few weeks after my dad passed away, my family and I experienced a flurry of typical RSPK in the house. By that time, I was versed enough in the paranormal to know what that was--and to theorize that it was not my dad himself who was making such a fuss, but that one of us he left behind was trying desperately to fill up with activity that newly empty space. Interestingly, after weeks of increasingly disturbing activity, my mom had me call a priest from our parish to come and bless the house. "I feel so silly," I told him on the phone. "Don't worry," he responded, "This happens all the time."

The young associate came over to dinner the next evening; during the meal, the racket from the second floor of the house was so disruptive that we put the dinner on hold while our priest went from room to room, blessing as he went.

You don't have to believe that this ritual ended our paranormal phenomena because my dad was there and the blessing helped him along to the Other Side, or because we believed he was, and that it would. But, that evening, peace was restored to our house. We enjoyed the rest of our dinner, said goodbye to our understanding priest, and went to bed. Our family home has never been bothered by "ghosts" again.

To this day, I don't know if it was my dad or our own depression that suddenly haunted our house almost twenty years ago, and I don't know what un-haunted it, either. And I guess that's why I'm still doing this, isn't it?

Mark Nesbitt

Mark Nesbitt was born in Lorain, Ohio, and graduated from Baldwin-Wallace College with a BA in English Literature. He is a former National

Park Service Ranger/Historian. He started his own research and writing company in 1977 He has conducted historical research, and created advertising copy, for some of America's leading historical artists. His books include *Drummer Boy at Gettysburg* (1977), *If the South Won Gettysburg* (1980),*35 Days to Gettysburg* (1992), *Rebel Rivers* (1993), *Saber and Scapegoat: J.E.B. Stuart and the Gettysburg Controversy* (1994), *Through Blood and Fire* (1996), and the best selling *Ghosts of Gettysburg* Series (1991- present). His stories have been seen, and/or heard, on The History Channel, A&E, The Travel Channel, Unsolved Mysteries, Coast to Coast AM, regional television and radio programs, and in local newspapers and publications. He has been a keynote speaker for the Virginia House of Delegates, The Lotos Literary Club of New York, the Capital Area Intermediate Unit of the Teaching American History Project, the Baltimore Paranormal Convention, Pennsylvania Paranormal Conventions, the New Jersey Ghost Conference, and numerous local Civil War Roundtables.

Mark was awarded the 1977-78 Eastern National Park and Monument Association's National Award for Excellence in a Children's Publication. In July of 2004, his *Ghosts of Gettysburg* Series received the National Paranormal Award for "Best True Hauntings Collection" and "Best 'Local Haunt' Guidebook".

Stories from the *Ghosts of Gettysburg* Series spawned the commercially successful Ghosts of Gettysburg Candlelight Walking Tours® in 1994. From March through November, the ghost tours provide entertainment for visitors to Gettysburg, PA.

What does Mark say?

In 1991 Michael Talbot published *The Holographic Universe.* In it he suggests a model of the universe and reality as we know it as a giant hologram: "...there is evidence to suggest that our world and everything in it--from snowflakes to maple trees to falling stars and spinning electrons--are also only ghostly images, projections from a level of reality so beyond our own it is literally beyond both space and time."

Talbot uses this new paradigm of our universe to explain not only mountains and sub-atomic particles, but brings it to a personal level: how dreaming can be a bridge to this sub-strata of reality where we actually visit a parallel universe; how "miracles" like stigmata, or mass healings, or psychokinesis are produced by tapping into that level of reality.

Materializations and dematerializations of physical objects, too, are man-ifestations of another world co-existing with the one in which we "live." It may also be the place where "spirits" go to dwell until they choose to rein-carnate again into the visible, everyday reality.

Which brings us to a definition of "ghosts."

We know our visible, tangible world via the frequency of the energy waves-sound and light-we are able to receive from it. Most people, most of the time, can "receive" only the frequency of our visible world.

The other parallel frequency domain--the vast, universal energy field of which the personal, human energy field is a part--is resonating at a dif-ferent rate than that which we are used to, and so is also undetectable to most of us most of the time. But being a resonating energy field, we can also occasionally tune in to the frequency domain, like a radio tunes in to radio waves. Often this "tuning-in" happens by accident-accident of place or individual mood-and lends us a vision into the other world, a vision of a place, or thing, or person, out of time: a "ghost," or "ghostly experience."

If our personal, resonating energy field is part of an eternal, second-ary, underlying reality and all it takes is for us to be tuned to the right fre-quency to see into this alternate reality, it could mean there is now a key to the door into this other world. Some are fortunate enough to be able to tune into this field already-we call them "sensitives," or "psychics." But perhaps anyone, using the correct training, such as biofeedback, or even just plain practice, can, over time, learn to experience the wonders of the Other World.

Jack Roth

Jack Roth is a writer/photographer who resides in Orlando, Florida. Jack's strong interest in photography is what initially led him to Dr. Andrew Nichols and the world of the paranor-mal. While taking photographs at the Myrtles Plantation in St. Francisville, Louisiana, he dis-covered that he had captured paranormal images in his photographs. The discovery of these para-normal anomalies prompted him to contact Dr. Nichols. Since then, Jack has participated in var-ious investigations in New Orleans, where he produced and wrote a pilot episode for the TV series *Hauntings: A Journey Into the Unknown.*
He has carefully documented, both as a writer and photographer, a great deal of paranormal activity in the Crescent City. He has also acted as a field investigator for Dr. Nichols and the American Institute of Parapsychology (AIP), performing preliminary research into the authen-ticity of possible hauntings in cities such as Savannah (GA), Charleston

(SC), St. Augustine (FL), San Antonio (TX), DeLand (FL) and Orlando (FL). In February 2001, he completed filming a pilot for a new television series, *Ghost Detectives*, which aired in April 2001 on the Discovery Channel. He is currently working with Dr. Nichols on their first collaborative book effort, "Haunted Florida."

What does Jack say?

I've been involved with paranormal research for a decade now, and although I don't have any definitive answers to the mysteries of life and death, I've experienced enough to convince me that some form of human consciousness survives bodily death.

First, we need to differentiate between the various types of hauntings and rule out which ones do NOT involve discarnate entities. Having said that, I believe that poltergeists represent what scientists and researchers refer to as recurrent spontaneous psychokinesis, a function of the living mind and therefore not associated with discarnate entities. I do believe, however, that a psychic link exists between the living and the dead and that telepathy may very well play a part in how these phenomena are experienced.

Hauntings fall into two major categories, both of which define what a ghost might be.

The first is an imprint (or residual) haunting, which is when emotional events are imprinted on the environment in which they occurred. These recorded imprints are randomly projected from time to time, much like a movie, and living beings with the appropriate psychic capacity can pick up on various sights, sounds and smells associated with them. I firmly believe that imprint hauntings are real and that in time science (quantum physics) will bare this out. Although imprint hauntings do not suggest the existence of discarnate entities, they do provide us with the ability to witness history the way a time machine would. This in itself warrants serious research.

The second is a genuine haunting, which is when consciousness (or a fragment of consciousness) survives bodily death and attempts to communicate with the living in some manner. This suggests the existence of discarnate entities, spirits and survival of "life" after death. I've experienced nothing that would constitute proof of this but have accumulated enough compelling evidence that suggests it's a real possibility. Definitive proof of genuine hauntings may never be found, as it may not be meant for science to quantify such phenomena. Nevertheless, we need to continue in our quest for the truth.

Ray Couch

Ray Couch is a marketing/tourism expert who resides in Orlando, Florida. He grew up hearing his parents tell ghost stories from their home state of Kentucky, which peaked his interest in paranormal phenomena. As he began to research the phenomena, he discovered that his family has been having encounters with ghosts for generations. Ray's intuitive nature made him an immediate asset to the AIP as it began increasing field investigations in the Central Florida area. Ray has performed both preliminary and overnight investigations for the AIP in cities such as Orlando, DeLand, St. Augustine, Savannah, San Antonio and Kissimmee (FL). His ability to research historic properties and investigate reports of possible paranormal activity has led to the discovery of many great investigative sites. Ray hopes to publish a book on ghosts and paranormal phenomena that focuses on his personal experiences in the field.

What does Ray say?

I am not sure what a ghost is. I know that there is more than one type of ghost. I think it is like saying what is a human, and then seeing all the cultural differences in our own groups. I personally don't believe that they are the souls of the dead. I think most of them are residual energies; possibly they are memories that play themselves over and over. I believe that some are genuine ghosts and seem to contain a fragment of consciousness held together by an energy field. I have always felt that some could be explained by the theory of a so-called fourth dimension, and I feel even stronger about that since we [Vince and I] have been working together.

In Conclusion

I am sure that one week after this book goes to print, a new theory will emerge as to what ghosts might be or a new technique will be revealed in finding ghosts. That happened with *Ghost Tech*. As soon as my first book was in the press, I thought of three new pieces of ghost hunting technology I could have talked about in that book. I deliberately tried not mentioning any theories pertaining to what ghosts could be from a skeptical perspective since there are already quite a few books out there like that already. But, to be fair, I guess I could mention a few.

- Ghosts are figments of the imagination.
- They are hallucinations caused by stress or mental illness.
- Ghosts are hallucinations caused by low-level sound vibrations.
- Ghosts are hallucinations caused by electromagnetic fields.
- People who see ghosts are stupid.

Stupid, crazy or under the influence of EMF, which do you prefer?

I have not yet seen a ghost. I have experienced strange things that certainly hint at the existence of ghosts. I have recorded EVP and have taken some very weird pictures. I have heard unaccountable noises such as furniture being moved around that weren't and have even seen video with "something" on it that appears to be the transparent silhouette of a human form. In Gettysburg, I heard invisible footsteps in the battlefields and saw objects move without any explanation other than a paranormal one. Friends and colleagues who I trust wholeheartedly have shared similar experiences with me.

I believe them.

I truly believe that ghosts are real.

GHOST HUNTING DO'S & DON'TS

DO'S

- Read as much as can from as many sources as possible. Use common sense to sort out right from wrong.
- Catalog as much data as possible.
- File your data in a concise and easily searchable system.
- As much as you can, follow the scientific method for research.
- Learn from your mistakes.
- Forgive for mistakes made.
- A little obsession goes a long way.
- Remember, your ghost hunting team is also your part of your family.

DON'TS

- Don't let anyone on your team that will hold your team back.
- Don't let your friends and colleagues down.
- Don't fall into the trap of thinking you're going to make a lot of money from ghost investigating. You're not.
- Don't charge for investigations.
- Don't charge for sharing data. Yes... Some people do this.
- Don't ever stop believing!

Sincerely,
Vince Wilson

GHOST SCIENCE GLOSSARY

A

ASQ (pronounced "ask"): The three phases of an EVP investigation. Alone. Supervise. Ask.
1. Leave the recorder alone until the tape runs out.
2. Supervise the recording area while it records.
3. Ask questions to check for an intelligent haunting.

Atom: The smallest possible piece of any pure element that still has the properties of that element. Atoms are made of smaller particles including electrons, protons, and neutrons. Differences in the numbers of these particles create the differences between the elements. An atom is about 500-billionths of an inch, or one hundred millionths of a centimeter across. (As quoted by the PBS Glossary website)

B

Barometer: Any device that measures air pressure.

Black Hole: An object that has gravity so strong that not even light can escape from it. Has infinite density.

C

Chaos Theory: A branch of mathematics that studies long-term change, which is sensitive to initial conditions, so that small initial changes cause great differences long-term.

Clairvoyance: Seeing beyond normal sight. Sometimes called "second sight". See also ESP.

Classic Haunting: Also called an "Intelligent Haunting" or "Traditional Haunting"; rare, a sentient spirit that can manifest itself into an apparition and communicate with the living; the ghost responds to outside stimuli like questions and statements; it can be friendly or hostile and will let you know the difference; they are sometimes capable of opening and closing doors and windows and moving objects like furniture around.

D

Dogma: A blind belief in things to be unquestionably true, often without a material base.

Dynamical energy systems theory: Suggests that all dynamical systems store information and energy to various degrees.

E

EMF: Electromagnetic Field.

EMR: Electromagnetic Resonance.

Enticement Experiment/Technique: Using objects from different time periods (money, toys, antiques, etc.) or reenacting events from the past (playing poker in a haunted casino or shouting a roll call in a battlefield for example) to "entice" reactions from ghosts.

ESP (Extra-Sensory Perception): Paranormal abilities such as precognition, telepathy, and clairvoyance.

EVP (Electronic Voice Phenomena): The recording of spirit voices through electronic means.

F

Frequency: the number of times that the current goes through a complete cycle per second.

G

Gauss: the preferred unit in the United States for measuring magnetic field exposure; also the German mathematician who developed the theory of numbers and who applied mathematics to electricity and magnetism and astronomy and geodesy (1777-1855).

Ghost: From Anglo-Saxon gast, from a root word seen in Icelandic geisa, to rage as fire, and Swedish gusa, to ferment. Believed to be a remnant of the human consciousness.

H

Hall Effect: A way of measuring magnetic fields. A current in a suitable semiconductor experiences a sideways force, in turn creating a measurable voltage, proportional to the magnetic field.

Hawking Radiation: In physics, Hawking radiation is thermal radiation that is by black holes due to quantum effects. It is named after British physicist Stephen Hawking who worked out the theoretical argument for its existence in 1974. Hawking's discovery became the first convincing insight in quantum gravity. However, the existence of Hawking radiation remains controversial.

Hypercube: A higher dimensional object that is impossible for our 3D minds to visualize.

Hyperspace: Higher dimensional space.

I

Intelligent Haunting: see Classic Haunting.

K

Kinetic Energy: Energy possessed by a body in motion.

M

Memory Possession: Through electromagnetic resonance, or other means, a person is taken over or possessed by the memories of persons and/or events of the past. Someone experiencing a memory possession will experience one or more of the following:
1.   Emotional duress. You will feel emotions outside of what you felt before entering the "memory possession zone". The emotions can be pleasant or unpleasant.
2.   Feeling of being watched.
3.   Feeling of being touched. Many who have been in haunted locations have claimed physical sensations of being touched or handled. The question is, are you being touched or are you experiencing the sensation of someone from the past being handled?
4.   Witness of apparition(s). Are you witnessing a ghost manifest itself, or are you viewing the memories of someone from the past?
5.   Viewing of past events as eyewitness. In this more rare case of a very powerful memory possession a person will be completely immersed in events from the past. They may feel as if they are someone else and even hear another person's voice come from their mouth. Would be like a "waking dream". Ex.: A person walks in the fields of Gettysburg and is carried back over 140 years to the Battle of Gettysburg. The subject will take on the role of a soldier and will witness the battle as it takes place. They

will not have control over their actions in most cases and will literally "reenact" events that transpired. If the soldier's memories are of being shot, then the subject will feel the effect of being shot.

Molecule: Smallest portions of a substance having the properties of the substance.

P

Pareidolia: (from the Greek para- amiss, faulty, wrong and eidolon, diminutive of eidos appearance, form): Seeing defined objects in non-defined subjects. Example: seeing the Virgin Mary in a tree stump or the devil in a fireplace. Also called, although inaccurately, simulacra.

Platonist/Platonism: (As defined by Wikepedia.com) Platonic idealism is the theory that the substantive reality around us is only a reflection of a higher truth. That truth, Plato argues, is the abstraction. A particular tree, with a branch or two missing, possibly alive, possibly dead, and initials of two lovers carved into its bark, is distinct from the form of Tree-ness. A Tree is the ideal that each of us holds that allows us to identify the imperfect reflections of trees all around us.

Poltergeist Agent (PA): Phenomena usually surrounding a young child, which is usually a girl; the P.A. (the child) is almost always around when the poltergeist activity occurs; this usually involves objects being thrown around when there is no one around, unexplainable tapping and scratching noises and objects disappearing and reappearing hours, days or weeks later; in worst-case scenarios there can be injuries to human beings from thrown objects and scratches appearing on the flesh of the P.A.; fires are also known to occur in the worst cases - sometimes with catastrophic results.

Potential Energy: Energy that is stored; Energy of position or state.

Q

Quantum Mechanics: The well-tested theory of the behavior of matter on the microscopic scales of atoms and computer chips, where the subatomic particles that compose all matter behave simultaneously like waves and particles.

Quarks: Fundamental particles, incapable of independent existence, that combines to form particles such as protons and neutrons.

R

Radiation: Energy that is radiated or transmitted in the form of rays or waves or particles.

Residual Haunting: Probably the most common type of haunting; this is best described as an imprint on the environment; a moment in time, burnt onto the surroundings of a specific location; playing out roles and situations over and over again for centuries at a time; most researchers compare this to a looped video that repeats itself forever; in these cases you might hear footsteps and other strange noises; however, if you see the event being played out, you will not be able to interfere; the "ghosts" here are not conscience of their surroundings; they may not be sentient.

S

The Scientific Method: A systematic approach to observing phenomena, drawing conclusions and testing hypotheses. The scientific method follows a series of steps: (1) identify a problem you would like to solve, (2) formulate a hypothesis, (3) test the hypothesis, (4) collect and analyze the data, (5) make conclusions.

Semiconductor: A substance through which the flow of electricity can be controlled - its conductive properties are between those of a metal conductor and an insulator

Simulacra: (from Wikipedia.org): Simulacrum is a Latin word originally meaning a material object representing something (such as an idol representing a deity, or a painted still-life of a bowl of fruit). By the 1800s it developed a sense of a "mere" image, an empty form devoid of spirit, and descended to a specious or fallow representation.

In other words: Something that looks like something else done deliberately. (see also: Pareidolia)

Skeptic: Someone who habitually doubts accepted beliefs

Systemic: Pertaining to or affecting a system, such that the body or system is affected as a whole.

Systems Theory: Systems Theory sees our world in terms of 'systems', where each system is a 'whole' that is more than the sum of its parts, but also itself a 'part' of larger systems. For example, a cell is more than just a pile of molecules and itself is a part of larger systems e.g. an organ. An organ is on one level a whole in itself, but on another, it is a part of a system at the level of an individual person. A family and a community can both be seen as 'systems' where the 'parts' are people. (Taken from "What is Deep Ecology?" by Chris Johnstone)

T

Thermometer: any device used for measuring temperature

Traditional Haunting: see Classic Haunting.

Triple-axis meter: a type of EMF meter; uses three coils and three metal plates on an x, y, and z-axis; that way the user can read fields from three different directions; the metal plates detect AC or DC electric fields; each coil has a different calibration that lets you detect all angles instead of just the area in front of the device; on most models you can switch between each setting or, using a computer circuit, reads the sum of the magnetic and electric.

V

Voltage - The force that pushes electricity through a wire.

W

Worm Hole: A hypothetical shortcut through the space-time continuum. Also called an Einstein-Rosen bridge.

RECOMMENDED READING

Thinking about starting your own GHOST-HUNTING LIBRARY? Well, you're off to a great start! Allow me to suggest some other great books for anyone seriously interested in being taken seriously as a serious researcher of ghosts and hauntings!

Must have GHOST HUNTING books:

The Ghost Hunter's Guidebook by Troy Taylor

Do you believe in ghosts? Want to know how to find them? Then don't miss the new edition of Troy Taylor's ultimate guide to ghost research. This book is the essential guide to investigating ghosts and hauntings and in this updated and revised edition, the author not only expands the original material from the previous edition, but he also adds new information on investigation techniques, ghost detection equipment, cameras, researching haunted history and much more!

Ghost Tech by Vince Wilson

This entertaining and informative book offers a wealth of practical information on basic equipment operations, the ins and outs of using the equipment during investigations and much more. The book explores the nature of ghosts, temperature detection devices and how to use them, the uses and misuses of EMF meters, recording the voices of the dead, using cameras for investigations, recording the paranormal on video, various types of equipment and how to use it and much more! This is a must-have book for anyone with an interest in ghost research and the proper use of the scientific equipment that has become so prevalent in the supernatural field. It is an essential guide to paranormal research and the perfect addition to any ghost hunter's tool kit!

Ghosts on Film by Troy Taylor

Author and ghost researcher Troy Taylor once again delves into the supernatural with a guide to the history and mystery of spirit photography. In this latest installment in the popular "Haunted Field Guide" series, the author takes an in-depth look at the controversial and mysterious history of spirit photography, including a look at the mediums and scientists who pioneered the field and the most famous pictures that allege to be ghosts captured on film. The book also includes a detailed exploration of the way that cameras have impacted the field of paranormal research and a recounting of some of the best-known cases where cameras played a crucial role, as well as a detailed guide for using your own camera in ghost investigations. Other sections of the book feature an examination of how cameras capture ghostly images, the forms that paranormal energy takes, hints and tips on using cameras in ghost research, step by step guides to photographic investigations and chapters on analyzing photos, detecting photographic trickery, accidental photos, camera operations and much more!

The Field Guide to Haunted Graveyards by Troy Taylor

The book includes a detailed look at the American cemetery, as well as American burial customs and traditions and a how-to guide for conducting paranormal investigations in graveyards. Discover how to find the history of a particular cemetery, burial records, information from tombstones and grave markers, cemetery plats and maps, and much more. There are also case studies from haunted places, updated info on spirit photography and a state-by-state guide to haunted graveyards -- many of which have never appeared in print before! Over 200 graveyards are listed and reviewed. This is the first ever research guide for investigating cemetery ghosts and an essential addition to the library of any ghost enthusiast, paranormal investigator or cemetery buff!

The Encyclopedia of Ghosts and Spirits by Rosemary Ellen Guiley

Featuring more then 500 entries, The Encyclopedia of Ghosts and Spirits is a mesmerizing compendium of worldwide paranormal activity. With explanations of strange phenomena from both folklore and modern scientific research, it examines famous hauntings, historical figures and events, and myths and legends surrounding ghosts and spirits in different cultures. This edition covers recent breakthroughs and incidents, new information about important myths, and current research into ghosts and other paranormal occurrences. What's more, the forewords are by Tom Perrott, former Chairman of the Ghost Club and Troy Taylor, President of the American Ghost Society. Ghost hunters absolutely must have this book!

RECOMMENDED WEBSITES

The Barringer Crater
www.barringercrater.com/science/

Bible and History
www.piney.com

The Gallop Organization
www.gallup.com

The Center for Voice
www.voice.northwestern.edu

Craig Teleshe
www.ghost-tech.com

Ghosts of Gettysburg (Mark Nesbitt)
www.ghostsofgettysburg.com

Ghost Tech: The Official Site for Ghost Tech and
Ghost Science by Vincent Wilson
www.ghosttech.net

Google
www.google.com

History & Hauntings/Ghosts of the Prairie (Troy Taylor)
www.prairieghosts.com

Less EMF
www.lessemf.com

Loyd Auerbach
www.invisiblesignals.com and www.mindreader.com

The Maryland Paranormal Investigators Coalition
www.marylandparanormal.com

Nexus Magazine
www.nexusmagazine.com

Parapsychology Foundation, Inc.
www.parapsychology.org

PBS Glossary
http://www.pbs.org/transistor/glossary.html

Rick Fisher
www.paranormalpa.com

PhysLink.com
www.physlink.com

Sacred Texts
www.sacred-texts.com

The Science Company
www.sciencecompany.com

SMS.AC
www.sms.ac

Southern Ghosts
www.southernghosts.com and www.southernghostsradio.com

Space Weather
www.spaceweather.com

The Time Line Index
www.timelineindex.com

The Trickster and the Paranormal
www.tricksterbook.com

Visionary Living (Rosemary Ellen Guiley)
www.visionaryliving.com

Wikipedia
en.wikipedia.org

The Official Ghost Tech Website

Vince Wilson's Ghost Tech has expanded to the World Wide Web! Now you can go see what Vince couldn't fit into the books Ghost Tech and Ghost Science at **www.ghosttech.net.** Read articles and tips on ghost hunting and new experiments being conducted by Vince Wilson and the Maryland Paranormal Investigators Coalition. There will also be reviews on new technologies and articles by other ghost hunters from around the country. Don't forget to checkout the *Ghost Tech* Bookstore to jumpstart your ghost hunting library and the *Ghost Tech* Store where you can buy equipment and gear!

Also, download what are possibly the most comprehensive set of FREE ghost hunting forms in the country today! These forms are based on forms designed by Troy Taylor for his book *The Ghost Hunter's Guidebook,* including:

The Investigator Cover Form : This form is your cover sheet and will have your team member's names, base readings, number of visits to location, name and address of location, and a space for notes.

Room Grid Form: This form will allow you to document the location of hot spots and cold spots, artificial EMF locations, locations of furniture and obstructions and the room's reference point toward magnetic north.

Area Grid Form: This form is the same as the Room Grid Form except it is more detailed for outdoor investigations such as in cemeteries and battlefields. Mark the location of tombstones, monuments and trees.

Photo Log Form: This form will allow you to document where, when and why a photo was made. Who took the picture and if it was a new roll of film is also mentioned. We recommend using a 35mm camera.

Video Log Form: This form will help you with video surveillance. It will log up to 5 cameras (more if you use more than one form). It documents what type of camera, format of video, length of tape, location of camera, number of tapes used and reason for observation.

Room Data and Information Form 1: This form will help you document room temperature and humidity, EMF levels, electrical field readings and RF levels. Also documents the location in each room the readings were taken and at what time.

Room Data and Information Form 2: This form is much like the Room Data and Information Form 1 except it records cold spots, "strange feelings" (feeling of being watched, etc.) and "Other" readings with different types of devices.

We also have equipment like the ones we use on investigations for sale! Trifield meters and motions sensors are available as well as several other useful items!

BIBLIOGRAPHY

A Change of Heart, by Claire Sylvia and William Novak (1998)

The Concise Encyclopedia of Western Philosophy and Philosophers (1991)

Ghost Tech: The Essential Guide to Paranormal Investigation Equipment, by Vince Wilson (2005)

Ghosts on Film: The History, Mystery & How-to's of Spirit Photography, by Troy Taylor (2005)

The Encyclopedia of Ghosts and Spirits, by Rosemary Ellen Guiley (2000)

A Field Guide to Demons, Fairies, Fallen Angels, and Other Subversive Spirits, by Carol K. Mack and Dinah Mack (1999)

The Fourth Dimension: A Guided Tour of the Higher Universes, by Rudy Rucker (1984)

The Ghost Hunters Guidebook, by Troy Taylor (2004)

The Handy Science Answer Book, by the Science and Technology Department of Carnegie Library of Pittsburgh (2003)

Hyperspace: A Scientific Odyssey Through Parallel Universes, Time Warps, and the Tenth Dimension, by Michio Kaku, Robert O'Keefe (Illustrator) (1995)

In Search of Schrodinger's Cat: Quantum Physics and Reality, by John Gribbin (1984)

Parapsychology, Introduction to and Education in, by Parapsychology Foundation, Inc (1999)

Parapsychology: The Controversial Science, by Richard S. Broughton, Ph. D. (1991)

What is Deep Ecology?, by Chris Johnstone (2002)

Special Thanks to:

Troy Taylor
Robbin Van Pelt
Renée Colianni
Rosemary Ellen Guiley
Brooke Tarran
Mary Duvall
Mark and Carol Nesbitt
Ray Couch
Jack Ross
John and Kelly Weaver
And all the ghost hunters and authors who submitted content to the 'Theories from the Pros' chapter!

Vince Wilson created all original artwork for this book.
The author and publisher are in no way related or affiliated to Warner Brothers, Inc. or Warner Bros. Home Video.

Note from the Publisher: Although Whitechapel Productions Press, Vince Wilson, and all affiliated with this book have carefully researched all sources to insure the accuracy of the information contained in this book, we assume no responsibility for errors, inaccuracies or omissions.

ABOUT THE AUTHOR

Vince has always been interested in science, history and the unexplained since as far back as he can remember. Lingering around in the back of his mind for over a year he was inspired to finally create a group of paranormal investigators with an invested interest in serious research into the paranormal. The inspiration came from his long time friend from high school, Renée Hamer (Colianni). Together they founded the Baltimore Society for Paranormal Research. However, that would not be enough...

Vince found that there were so many organizations in Maryland that were not exactly 'professional' that it was hard to gain ground in the field. When colleagues from other states heard he was from Maryland, they generally rolled their eyes sarcastically. Maryland, one of the most haunted areas around, had a bad rep for paranormal research! That is when he founded the Maryland Paranormal Investigators Coalition. A group of groups dedicated to serious paranormal research and scientific observation.

Their mission statement:
- To provide leadership in Maryland through the application of scientific research of the paranormal.
- To provide education, assistance and resources to new and existing paranormal organizations, the public and the media.
- To foster and create new paranormal organizations throughout Maryland.

With the help of what he considers "the best bunch of paranormal researchers around" he has gotten some headway in the difficult task of turning around Maryland's reputation.

Vince is the author of *Ghost Tech*: The Essential Guide to the Equipment used by Paranormal Investigators. He has lectured on ghost hunting technology and is listed in the latest edition of Troy Taylor's *Ghost Hunter's Guidebook* and his book *Ghosts on Film* and Ed Okonowicz's *Baltimore Ghosts*. Vince wrote an article for Baltimore in Jeff Belanger's *The Encyclopedia of Haunted Places* and has also written for *Ghost Magazine*. He has appeared on all the major local TV stations in the Baltimore area and on numerous radio stations in regards to his work in paranormal research.

Vince has also appeared on *Creepy Canada* in 2005 for the *USS Constellation* and the Discovery Channel in 2006 for an investigation he did at the Edgar Allan Poe House in Baltimore.

He lives in a possibly haunted location in Southeast Baltimore (he refuses to investigate his own house) with his cats Monty, Teddy and Tucker.

Printed in the United States
67560LVS00001B/100-111

9 781892 523457